COMBATTING TERRORIST TRAVEL: DOES THE VISA WAIVER PROGRAM KEEP OUR NATION SAFE?

HEARING

BEFORE THE

SUBCOMMITTEE ON BORDER AND MARITIME SECURITY

OF THE

COMMITTEE ON HOMELAND SECURITY HOUSE OF REPRESENTATIVES

ONE HUNDRED FOURTEENTH CONGRESS

FIRST SESSION

MARCH 17, 2015

Serial No. 114–8

Printed for the use of the Committee on Homeland Security

Available via the World Wide Web: http://www.gpo.gov/fdsys/

U.S. GOVERNMENT PUBLISHING OFFICE

94–579 PDF   WASHINGTON : 2015

For sale by the Superintendent of Documents, U.S. Government Publishing Office
Internet: bookstore.gpo.gov   Phone: toll free (866) 512–1800; DC area (202) 512–1800
Fax: (202) 512–2104   Mail: Stop IDCC, Washington, DC 20402–0001

COMMITTEE ON HOMELAND SECURITY

MICHAEL T. MCCAUL, Texas, *Chairman*

LAMAR SMITH, Texas
PETER T. KING, New York
MIKE ROGERS, Alabama
CANDICE S. MILLER, Michigan, *Vice Chair*
JEFF DUNCAN, South Carolina
TOM MARINO, Pennsylvania
STEVEN M. PALAZZO, Mississippi
LOU BARLETTA, Pennsylvania
SCOTT PERRY, Pennsylvania
CURT CLAWSON, Florida
JOHN KATKO, New York
WILL HURD, Texas
EARL L. "BUDDY" CARTER, Georgia
MARK WALKER, North Carolina
BARRY LOUDERMILK, Georgia
MARTHA MCSALLY, Arizona
JOHN RATCLIFFE, Texas

BENNIE G. THOMPSON, Mississippi
LORETTA SANCHEZ, California
SHEILA JACKSON LEE, Texas
JAMES R. LANGEVIN, Rhode Island
BRIAN HIGGINS, New York
CEDRIC L. RICHMOND, Louisiana
WILLIAM R. KEATING, Massachusetts
DONALD M. PAYNE, JR., New Jersey
FILEMON VELA, Texas
BONNIE WATSON COLEMAN, New Jersey
KATHLEEN M. RICE, New York
NORMA J. TORRES, California

BRENDAN P. SHIELDS, *Staff Director*
JOAN V. O'HARA, *General Counsel*
MICHAEL S. TWINCHEK, *Chief Clerk*
I. LANIER AVANT, *Minority Staff Director*

————

SUBCOMMITTEE ON BORDER AND MARITIME SECURITY

CANDICE S. MILLER, Michigan, *Chairman*

LAMAR SMITH, Texas
MIKE ROGERS, Alabama
JEFF DUNCAN, South Carolina
LOU BARLETTA, Pennsylvania
WILL HURD, Texas
MARTHA MCSALLY, Arizona
MICHAEL T. MCCAUL, Texas *(ex officio)*

FILEMON VELA, Texas
LORETTA SANCHEZ, California
SHEILA JACKSON LEE, Texas
BRIAN HIGGINS, New York
NORMA J. TORRES, California
BENNIE G. THOMPSON, Mississippi *(ex officio)*

PAUL L. ANSTINE, *Subcommittee Staff Director*
DEBORAH JORDAN, *Subcommittee Clerk*
ALISON NORTHROP, *Minority Subcommittee Staff Director*

CONTENTS

COMBATTING TERRORIST TRAVEL: DOES THE VISA WAIVER PROGRAM KEEP OUR NATION SAFE?

Tuesday, March 17, 2015

U.S. HOUSE OF REPRESENTATIVES,
COMMITTEE ON HOMELAND SECURITY,
SUBCOMMITTEE ON BORDER AND MARITIME SECURITY,
Washington, DC.

The subcommittee met, pursuant to call, at 10:00 a.m., in Room 311, Cannon House Office Building, Hon. Candice S. Miller [Chairman of the subcommittee] presiding.

Present: Representatives Miller, Barletta, Hurd, McSally, Vela, Jackson Lee, and Torres.

Mrs. MILLER. The Committee on Homeland Security, our Subcommittee on Border and Maritime Security, will come to order. The subcommittee is meeting today to examine the Visa Waiver Program and its effect on terrorist travel.

We are pleased today to be joined by Dr. Marc Frey of the Steptoe Johnson law firm, Mr. Roger Dow of the U.S. Travel Association, Dr. Steven Bucci of the Heritage Foundation, and Mr. Brian Michael Jenkins of the RAND Corporation. I will formally introduce them in just a moment. But I would like to make my opening statement first, myself and the Ranking Member.

Over the past year, the Islamic State of Iraq and the Levant or ISIL and several other extremist groups have attracted tens of thousands of young men and women to join their ranks; many of whom hold passports in France, the United Kingdom, Belgium, Canada, and other Western nations, including United States. Many foreign fighters could be just one flight away, bringing with them the skills, training, ideology, and commitment to killing Americans that they have learned overseas.

The threat that these foreign fighters pose is significant and growing in large part because the terrorists with Western passports are eligible for visa-free travel to the United States through the Visa Waiver Program. If we do not have good intelligence on the travel of these fighters or our allies in the Visa Waiver Program are not appropriately sharing what they know, then U.S. citizens could be at risk.

Last year, this subcommittee held a hearing on the Visa Waiver Program, where we heard from Government witnesses. We have called this hearing today to get an independent look at this program from outside experts. The Visa Waiver Program was designed to facilitate travel, to reduce the burden on the State Department,

(1)

and to help encourage travel to the United States. However, after the tragic events of September 11, 2001, the program evolved to be a significant counterterrorism tool by simultaneously facilitating legitimate trade and travel.

Now, let me just state from the outset that I believe that this program is very effective at both facilitating travel and increasing our National security. Through the addition of the Electronic System for Travel Authorization—that we call ESTA—the information that CBP knows about a traveler before they get on a plane significantly increases our security.

Some of my colleagues have called for the Visa Waiver Program to be canceled or suspended. I personally think that is misguided. Millions of travelers fly using VWP every year, and stopping this program would bring cost to our economy and CBP would lose an important source of information for screening travelers entering the United States. In addition, information-sharing agreements, which are a prerequisite for membership, are also a key part of the intelligence that keeps Americans safe.

Make no mistake, terrorists are indeed looking for weaknesses in our defenses, and we have to prevent them from succeeding. Rather than end this valuable program, we need to continually evaluate the program to make sure it adequately balances our economic and security needs, especially in the light of the growing threat of foreign fighters entering the United States. Expansion of the program should only be done when it aligns with the security and economic interests of the United States, once a viable biometric exit system is in place, which can lead to more accurate reporting of visa overstay rates by our country.

To that end, I continue to call on this administration to publically release visa overstay rates, which are currently obtained through the flawed biographic system. While I am not surprised by the administration's lack of transparency on this, I am disappointed. The visa overstay report was promised to this Congress by Secretary Napolitano. While complete, the report continues to be held up by the White House. I urge the release of this report. The delay only serves to reinforce our belief that a biometric system would produce more timely and accurate results and could lead to expansion of this program for some of our Nation's most trusted allies.

Earlier this year, I introduced H.R. 158, the Visa Waiver Program Improvement Act that I believe will help to minimize the ability of terrorists to exploit the program. The bill allows the Secretary of Homeland Security to suspend participation of countries in the VWP if they do not share critical terrorism and foreign traveler data with the United States consistent with the program's underlying agreements.

This bill also requires the Department of Homeland to consider collecting additional pieces of information on ESTA applications to better screen foreign travelers, and requires an annual intelligence assessment conducted by the director of national intelligence and DHS to assess airport, passport, and travel document standards. This sounds like common sense. I think it is. Was very pleased that Secretary Johnson also called for adding of additional data elements to the ESTA application in November after this bill was initially introduced that called for a look at additional data elements to be considered.

Although CBP continuously vets all visa and ESTA applicants against our terrorist holdings, that information is imperfect if we do not have a complete picture of an individual's travel route. Collecting more information up-front will be helpful to do just that. Critical information sharing, especially with our European allies, is vital to help combat the threat of foreign fighters bound for the United States.

Unfortunately, Europe as a whole has been reluctant sometimes to share certain passenger name record data or PNR data with the United States, and such a gap puts United States citizens at risk. We recently learned that it was only after a prominent terrorist attack overseas that a Visa Waiver country provided the Department of Homeland Security names of individuals which pose a terror concern. Some of the names shared were not even on our radar screen previously.

Unfortunately, this demonstrates that we still have an information-sharing problem with some of our closest allies. Our bill gives the Department of Homeland the leverage it needs to make sure the information critical to our homeland security is being shared appropriately. As we have noted on many occasions, the 9/11 Commission was crystal-clear on this point when they said for terrorists, travel documents are as important as weapons.

So I certainly look forward to hearing from our witness today on the value of the Visa Waiver Program and what further changes we should look at to strengthen the Visa Waiver Program to combat the threat of foreign fighters. This subcommittee has a long record of interest and oversight when it comes to visa and travel document security. The reason for that, obviously, is very clear. Many terrorist plots and attacks have been successful or nearly successful because of holes in our visa and border security defenses. Defeating terrorists' ability to move internationally has long been a focus area for this subcommittee. There certainly is more that we can do and need to do to prevent attacks and limit terrorist mobility. That is the purpose of our hearing today.

The Chairman now recognizes the Ranking Minority of this subcommittee, the gentleman from Texas, Mr. Vela. Let me just mention that I am very, very delighted to have him serve as the Ranking Member. I certainly am looking forward to working very closely with him as we go through the 114th Congress on issues of bipartisan concern. There is nothing more concerning, certainly, than providing for the common defense, which is actually in the preamble of our Constitution, and is a principle reason for this committee. Thank you.

Mr. VELA. I agree, Chairman Miller, that this issue is one that has bipartisan support, because we all know how important it is to protect our country against terrorism. I want to thank you for holding today's hearing regarding the security of Visa Waiver Program.

As Chairman Miller and I both represent border districts with maritime interests, albeit on different borders, I believe we have many areas of mutual interest and concern to address in our work as this subcommittee moves forward.

Today, we are focusing on a border security issue of a different kind than what we are used to discussing; the security of a program that facilitates the travel of millions of visitors to this country each year, the Visa Waiver Program. In fact, with 38 countries currently participating in the program, about 40 percent of all overseas visitors enter the United States without a visa pursuant to the Visa Waiver Program.

Unfortunately, there is a growing concern that the Visa Waiver Program could be exploited by terrorists, and particularly those holding Western passports, who could attempt to travel to this country under this program.

With direction and support from Congress, in recent years the Department of Homeland Security has worked to strength the security of the Visa Waiver Program through the Electronic System for Travel Authorization and its other predeparture passenger screening programs. These programs complement and are supported by information-sharing agreements with Visa Waiver Program partnerships—partners that provide Department of Homeland Security with data to vet travelers more effectively.

With thousands of foreign fighters traveling to and from Syria, some of whom hold Western passports, concerns about the security of the Visa Waiver Program are not entirely unfounded. I hope our witnesses can share with us their perspectives on whether the Visa Waiver Program is secure or if Congress and the Department of Homeland Security need to do more to shore up this very important program.

As a Member representing a border district, I am keenly aware of the importance of international travel and trade to our Nation and its economy. I believe I join many of my colleagues in the hope that we can find a way to ensure the security of the Visa Waiver Program, while continuing to welcome visitors under the program to the United States.

Again, I thank the witnesses for joining us. I look forward to our discussion today and to a productive Congress for this subcommittee.

[The statement of Ranking Member Vela follows:]

STATEMENT OF RANKING MEMBER FILEMON VELA

MARCH 17, 2015

Thank you for holding today's hearing regarding the security of the Visa Waiver Program (VWP).

As Chairman Miller and I both represent border districts with maritime interests, albeit on different borders, I believe we have many areas of mutual interest and concern to address in our work.

Today, we are focusing on a border security issue of a different kind than what we are used to discussing—the security of a program that facilitates the travel of millions of visitors to this country each year, the Visa Waiver Program (VWP).

In fact, with 38 countries currently participating in the program, about 40 percent of all overseas visitors enter the United States without a visa pursuant to the VWP.

Unfortunately, there is growing concern that the VWP could be exploited by terrorists, and particularly those holding Western passports, who could attempt to travel to this country under program.

With direction and support from Congress, in recent years DHS has worked to strengthen the security of the VWP, through the Electronic System for Travel Authorization (ESTA) and its other pre-departure passenger screening programs.

These programs complement and are supported by information-sharing agreements with VWP partners that provide DHS with data to vet travelers more effectively.

Still, with thousands of foreign fighters traveling to and from Syria, some of whom hold Western passports, concerns about the security of the VWP are not entirely unfounded.

I hope our witnesses can share with us their perspectives on whether the VWP is secure, or if Congress and DHS need to do more to shore up this important program.

As a Member representing a border district, I am keenly aware of the importance of international travel and trade to our Nation and its economy.

I believe I join many of my colleagues in the hope that we can find a way to ensure the security of the VWP while continuing to welcome visitors under the program to the United States.

Mrs. MILLER. Thank you very much.

Other Members of the committee are reminded that opening statements may be submitted for the record.

[The statement of Ranking Member Thompson follows:]

STATEMENT OF RANKING MEMBER BENNIE G. THOMPSON

MARCH 17, 2015

I would also like to thank the witnesses for appearing today to testify about the Visa Waiver Program (VWP) and its implications for our Nation's security. Since its establishment in the wake of the terrorist attacks of 9/11, this committee has been actively engaged in helping to address the threat of terrorist travel. Our focus has included addressing the potential security vulnerabilities of the VWP and ways to prevent terrorists from exploiting the program.

For example, as Chairman I authored a key provision of the 9/11 Act requiring the implementation of an Electronic System for Travel Authorization (ESTA) to provide DHS with more information about VWP travelers prior to their departure for the United States.

From the inception of the ESTA program in August 2008, CBP has approved over 80 million ESTAs but denied over 4,300 applications as a result of vetting against the Terrorist Screening Database. Also, CBP has denied over 35,000 applications for individuals who applied for an ESTA using a passport reported lost or stolen.

Recently, the VWP has been the subject of renewed attention due to concerns about the potential threat posed by foreign fighters with the Islamic State of Iraq and the Levant (ISIL), and particularly those holding Western passports who could attempt to travel under the VWP.

In response to this foreign fighter threat, late last year DHS took the step of enhancing the ESTA program by requiring travelers to provide additional data elements on their ESTA applications. This additional data allows DHS to better vet VWP travelers prior to departure to the United States, in turn better securing the VWP. It is imperative that DHS and their Federal partners continue to work with Congress to identify and address any new or outstanding vulnerabilities within the VWP. At the same time, it is important not to focus exclusively on Western foreign fighters and the VWP such that we lose sight of other individuals who may seek to do us harm via othermeans.

Finally, we should remain mindful that the overwhelming majority of travelers to the United States, whether under the VWP or otherwise, are legitimate travelers coming to this country for business or pleasure. About 19 million people from VWP countries visited the United States in fiscal year 2012, accounting for 40 percent of all international visitors. We welcome their visits, embrace the cultural exchange, and recognize their important contributions to America's economy.

Today, I look forward to hearing from the witnesses about their perspectives on VWP as it currently exists, and whether the program can be made more secure while continuing to allow us to welcome visitors from around the world.

Mrs. MILLER. Again, as I mentioned, we are pleased to be joined by four distinguished witnesses to discuss today's very important issue.

First of all, Dr. Marc Frey is a senior director in the Washington office of Steptoe and Johnson, which is an international law firm. Prior to joining Steptoe, Dr. Frey held several senior positions at the Department of Homeland Security, including the director of the Visa Waiver Program from 2007 to 2010. In that role, he oversaw the development and implementation of the VWP and directed the successful effort to enhance its security futures. Dr. Frey also serves as a senior associate with the Center for Strategic and International Studies and is a member of the American Council on Germany and the Atlantic Council of the United States. We welcome you, sir.

Mr. Roger Dow is the president and CEO of the U.S. Travel Association, the National association representing all segments of travel if the United States. In this role, Mr. Dow leads U.S. travel efforts to advocate for improved travel facilitation and visa reform and to provide travel research and analysis. We welcome you, sir.

Dr. Steven P. Bucci is the director of the Doug and Sarah Allison Center for Foreign and National Security Policy Studies at the Heritage Foundation, a position that he has held since 2012. Prior to working at the Heritage Foundation, Dr. Bucci spent many years in the military, including service as the commander of the 3rd Battalion, 5th Special Forces. In 2001, he assumed his position as military assistant to Secretary Donald Rumsfeld in the Pentagon, where he was stationed on the terrorist attacks of September 11. We welcome you. Thank you for your service to this Nation.

Mr. Brian Michael Jenkins is a senior adviser to the president of the RAND Corporation and author of numerous books, reports, and articles on terrorism and terrorism-related topics. Mr. Jenkins is also a decorated combat veteran, having served with the 5th Special Forces Group in Vietnam. Welcome home. In 1996, Mr. Jenkins was appointed to the White House Commission on aviation safety and security. From 1999 to 2000, he served as adviser to the National Commission on Terrorism. In 2000, was appointed to the U.S. Comptroller General's Advisory Board. So our witnesses' full statement will appear in the record.

The Chairman now recognizes Dr. Frey for his testimony.

STATEMENT OF MARC E. FREY, SENIOR DIRECTOR, STEPTOE AND JOHNSON, LLP

Mr. FREY. Thank you, Chairman Miller. Good morning. It is my pleasure to be here this morning to talk about the Visa Waiver Program and be part of this distinguished panel.

I think to start off, what I would like to say is—and I guess this is a good way to start off—is to agree with you and agree with the Ranking Member to answer the question that the hearing's title posed, does the Visa Waiver Program keep us safe? I think answer to that is unequivocally yes. It is a critical counterterrorism and security tool for the United States that also facilitates travel. I would like to spend a little bit of time this morning talking specifically about why that is.

Because as you also mentioned, this is a timely hearing. Given the threats we are facing today from foreign fighters in particular, it is our responsibility to continue to evaluate programs like the VWP to continue to ensure that they are meeting the current threat environment. The good news with respect to the VWP in particular is there is a history of Congress and the Executive branch doing just that; working together to periodically reform and modernize the program to adapt to current threats. The most significant reform, and the one that is the basis for most of what we will be talking about today, was the reforms implemented in 2007 under the 9/11 Commission Act, which produced ESTA, produced information-sharing agreements and other things we will go into.

But before doing that, I would like to, you know, take a little bit of time just to talk about what the Visa Waiver Program is and, perhaps equally important, what it isn't. Because there does seem to be a perception, as I think you also said, Chairman Miller, that these people are just one flight away. In one sense that is, of course, true. But a statement like that obscures all of the work and all of the screening that DHS in particular and CBP and other agencies in the U.S. Government do to make sure that we are vetting Visa Waiver Program travelers appropriately.

So when the Visa Waiver Program waives the consular interview portion, it makes up for it with a whole host of other security requirements. One of these, of course, is ESTA, the Electronic System for Travel Authorization, which we have talked about, which does individualized prescreening and vetting of Visa Waiver Program travelers. That vetting is recurrent. So it is not that you get your ESTA and then you are good for the eligibility period. It is that ESTA continually vets applicants' data against lists and derogatory information, and ESTAs can can be revoked if new information comes to light.

The second piece of the Visa Waiver Program that is important in this context is the information-sharing and intelligence-sharing agreements that we talked about. Those are particularly important because the benefit or the information that the United States Government receives from those agreements, is fed into the ESTA vetting process. So that ensures to the extent we can that we have as much information on bad actors in foreign countries that we need to do our screening.

But there are two other parts that I think are also worth mentioning as to why the Visa Waiver Program helps keep us safe and is a key security program. The first of these is secure passports. The Visa Waiver Program mandates that travelers travel on electronic passports. These are passports that contain the biometric chip that also have the information, a digital paragraph, increasingly fingerprints, that matches the bio page. These are much, much harder to forge and to use fraudulently than regular passports. It is only within the context of the VWP that travelers are required to use these. So we have a much better confirmation of identity.

The other piece that I think is worth talking about are the regular DHS-led audits of Visa Waiver Program countries. It is a pretty—having led and participated in a number of these audits, it is a pretty remarkable tool that allows a team of DHS experts, supplemented by personnel from other agencies as appropriate, to visit a country and spend up to a week or 10 days or so reviewing security standards, border security standards, aviation security standards, passport standards, talking to their counterterrorism and security and law enforcement officials, and really giving U.S. Government visibility into the security practices of these countries.

To the extent the Department finds particular issues or items that are not up to our standards, mitigation measures can be both recommended and, in certain cases, insisted upon. It is a collaborative effort. But it is one where we have a remarkable insight into how other countries do their security, including in this context how other countries are able to both identify and track potential radicalized individuals who may become foreign fighters.

So in that sense, it is a very powerful tool. Those four elements really do work together to make the Visa Waiver Program important and an important security tool. That said, it can be evaluated. It should be evaluated, as we are doing today. So I think this hearing serves an excellent purpose. I think some of the reforms in the Visa Waiver Improvement Act of 2015 meet that objective. As you said, they are sensible reforms. They are things DHS should be looking at. In some cases, they are things that DHS is doing already. I think that should be encouraged.

I look forward to answering more of your questions going forward about the program and about the H.R. 158, the Visa Waiver Improvement Act, in particular. Thank you.

[The prepared statement of Mr. Frey follows:]

PREPARED STATEMENT OF MARC E. FREY

MARCH 17, 2015

Thank you Chairman Miller, Ranking Member Vela, and Members of the subcommittee, for this opportunity to testify on the Visa Waiver Program (VWP) and its important role in keeping our Nation safe and secure. My name is Marc Frey. I am a senior director at Steptoe & Johnson LLP, an international law firm. Prior to joining Steptoe I served in several positions at the Department of Homeland Security (DHS), including as director of the Visa Waiver Program. In that role I oversaw the successful effort to enhance the security of and expand the VWP and managed the security assessments of member countries.

The unequivocal answer to the question posed by in the title of this hearing is "Yes." The Visa Waiver Program enhances U.S. security and is a critical element of the layered border security approach the United States has implemented since September 11, 2001. The VWP helps to ensure that our country remains open for travel and trade while preventing terrorists and criminals from crossing our border.

Following the terrorist attacks in Paris earlier this year commentators have speculated on the possibility of an attack on U.S. soil by terrorists possessing passports from France or other VWP countries. Many in the media and elsewhere labor under the misapprehension that security standards are looser for VWP travelers than for those traveling with a visa, and that this poses a threat to U.S. security. Concerns have been raised, for example, about the ability of foreign fighters with "Western" passports to enter the United States under the VWP by circumventing the consular interview.

Under the VWP, DHS waives the "B" nonimmigrant visa requirement for aliens traveling from the 38 approved countries, permitting stays of up to 90 days for business or tourism. A consular interview is not required. But, that does not mean that DHS waives security requirements for these travelers. To the contrary, the Department mandates additional, more stringent security requirements, for both the individual traveler and his or her home country. The result is a system that today provides as much security against terrorist or criminal travelers as the visa system.

Like any successful security program, VWP has been closely reviewed over the years, periodically undergoing reform and modernization to ensure that it responded to emerging threats and challenges. In the face of today's complex and persistent threat environment, we can and should identify ways to ensure the VWP's security standards remain robust. The "Visa Waiver Program Improvement Act of 2015" (H.R. 158) includes a number of provisions that further this objective.

EVOLUTION OF THE VWP

Since its inception in the late 1980s, the VWP has evolved into an essential tool for increasing global security standards, advancing information sharing, strengthening international relationships, and promoting legitimate trade and travel to the United States. Over the past decade in particular, Congress and the Executive branch have worked together to implement a number of enhancements to the VWP to address evolving threats to international travel and to the United States homeland. Therefore, although critics of the VWP often continue to cite the example of the "Shoe Bomber" Richard Reid, who as a British citizen traveled under the VWP in December 2001, the measures put in place over the past dozen years have successfully addressed this risk to date.

For example, in 2003 new requirements were put in place to tighten passport security standards for VWP travelers and to increase the frequency with which countries are formally reviewed for their designation status. Furthermore, in order to align with the recommendations of the 9/11 Commission, Congress mandated additional security requirements to VWP, including standards for secure travel documents, individualized pre-screening of travelers, bilateral information-sharing arrangements, prompt reporting of lost and stolen passports, and a threat assessment conducted by the director of national intelligence. Appropriately, these changes were enacted as part of the Secure Travel and Counterterrorism Partnership Act of 2007.

KEY SECURITY COMPONENTS OF THE VWP

As described below, the VWP enhances U.S. security in four mutually reinforcing ways:
- It enables individualized and recurrent screening of travelers against law enforcement and security databases;
- It mandates bilateral and multilateral information and intelligence sharing;
- It requires secure passports to confirm identity; and
- It permits regular audits of the security standards of participating countries.

First, the VWP screens all travelers against multiple law enforcement and security databases, including the Terrorist Screening Database, before they depart for the United States. Using the on-line Electronic System for Travel Authorization (ESTA), a VWP traveler is required to provide biographic information (including name, date of birth, and passport number) as well as his or her destination address in the United States. The traveler is also required to answer questions regarding communicable diseases, arrests, convictions for certain crimes, and past history of visa revocation or deportation. In November 2014, DHS expanded the personal data required for an ESTA application, to include national identity numbers for those who have them and data from a second passport if that passport is not from a VWP country, among other data elements. As a result, ESTA functions as a powerful screening tool, enabling recurrent, individualized vetting of travelers. Travelers without an ESTA approval cannot board a flight to the United States.

Second, the VWP mandates robust information and intelligence sharing between the United States and its VWP partners, including agreements to share information on known or potential terrorists and criminals and to report lost and stolen passport (LASP) data to INTERPOL. Supplementing the U.S. Government's "watch lists" and other databases with these three pieces of information from a traveler's home government greatly enhances DHS's ability to identify and stop travelers who pose a threat. Likewise, information the United States provides VWP member countries under these agreements helps their governments identify and disrupt terrorist and criminal travel to, from, and within their own borders.

Third, all VWP travelers must use secure travel documents that meet internationally recognized standards, which allows for easier detection of forged or fraudulent passports. The majority of VWP travelers are required to use electronic passports (e-passports), which have an embedded chip that includes the bearer's biometric information.[1] At the port of entry, the biographic and biometric data contained in the electronic chip is compared to both the traveler and the travel document being presented. There are many other layers of technical security in the e-passport production process and the document itself that make duplication or forgery much less likely.

Lastly, VWP countries are required to undergo periodic eligibility reviews designed to ensure that VWP membership does not compromise U.S. security, law enforcement, and immigration enforcement interests. These comprehensive assessments are conducted by DHS, with the assistance of other U.S. Government agencies as appropriate. Critically, these reviews involve a site visit during which a team of U.S. Government subject-matter experts examines the country's security and law enforcement capabilities and procedures. Among other issues, a site visit focuses on

---

[1] All passports issued after October 26, 2006, presented by aliens entering under the VWP must be electronic passports.

the existence of radicalized groups in the country and the government's efforts to address this concern. The findings from the site visit form the core of the comprehensive DHS evaluation of a country's fitness to continue participating in the VWP. Should DHS identify any issues or concerns during the course of its review, it can flag them for follow-up and/or propose and insist on mitigation measures.

To complement these reviews and to ensure recommended mitigation measures are carried out, DHS has developed a vigorous monitoring process to ensure awareness of changing conditions in VWP countries. This monitoring process includes regular consultation with U.S. law enforcement and intelligence agencies, as well as frequent communication with U.S. embassies abroad and foreign embassies in Washington for updates on law enforcement or security concerns related to the VWP. Overall, no other program provides the U.S. Government with the opportunity to conduct as far-reaching and consequential audits of foreign security standards, ensuring alignment with our high standards for managing risk.

Under current law, DHS has the authority to immediately terminate a country's membership if an emergency occurs in the country that threatens the law enforcement or security interest of the United States. The director of national intelligence is also able to recommend immediate suspension to DHS if any current and credible threat poses an imminent danger to the United States or its citizens and originates from a country participating in the VWP. H.R. 158 helpfully supplements these authorities by providing explicitly for program suspension should DHS, in consultation with the State Department, determine that a member country is not meeting its information-sharing obligations.

That the modernized VWP enhances U.S. security is widely recognized by security experts across the political spectrum. The last three secretaries of homeland security, for example, have praised the program's contribution to U.S. and international security. Indeed, for precisely that same reason, both the Bush and Obama administrations have added countries to the VWP. The VWP's security components make so much sense, in fact, that they are setting global standards for countering terrorist travel. A September 2014 U.N. Security Council Resolution on security measures to better track and deter terrorist travel activity reflects practices the VWP has enforced for member countries since 2008.

THE VWP AND U.S. BORDER SECURITY

Because of its strong security components, the VWP has become an integral part of the U.S. Government's ability to identify security or other risks associated with travelers at the earliest possible point and push-out our "virtual" border. In particular, the VWP helps answer the three key questions necessary to implement an effective risk-based border screening system:

- "Who is a threat?"—U.S. officials need to identify known and suspected terrorists as well as other individuals who may pose a threat.
- "Is the person coming to the United States?"—U.S. officials need to know, as early as possible, if the traveler should be examined more closely.
- "Is the person really who he says he is?"—U.S. officials determine if the traveler is presenting fraudulent documents.

Who Is a Threat?

The U.S. Government collects and maintains an array of information designed to identify those associated with terrorism or other illicit activities. These "watch lists" use identifiers—primarily biographic-based, but increasingly incorporating biometrics—to support border-screening protocols and procedures. However, when it comes to identifying dangerous individuals from abroad, the U.S. Government is not the only, or necessarily the best, source of information. In fact, if you wanted to identify potentially dangerous individuals from a particular country, say the United Kingdom, your first stop would not be Washington; it would be London. Many European countries have rapidly growing ethnic and religious immigrant communities, a small minority of which has the potential to become radicalized. It makes sense then that the person's home country is the best source of information about which of its citizens or residents is most likely to pose a risk to the United States. This kind of unprecedented bilateral and multi-lateral information sharing mandated by the VWP, along with the routine audits and inspections made possible by the program improves the U.S. Government's overall ability to identify bad actors and activity.

Is the Person Coming to the United States?

DHS begins the screening process well before a potentially risky traveler reaches the U.S. border; in fact, DHS begins the process before the traveler even arrives at an airport through ESTA. In addition to the ESTA requirement for VWP travelers,

11

DHS requires airlines to provide a copy of their passenger manifests and data from their reservation files. This information—which applies to all travelers and is provided to DHS a minimum of 72 hours in advance—helps the agency determine who to allow on-board a U.S.-bound plane, who requires further screening and investigation upon arrival, and who should be turned away and referred to appropriate law enforcement personnel. These advance-screening measures give DHS a better, more informed understanding of who is coming to the United States.

Is the Person Really Who He Says He Is?

No amount of "watch listing" and passenger screening will detect terrorists if they are able to travel on an assumed identity with fraudulently obtained or fake documents. In order to verify that people are who they say they are when they travel, DHS insists on high standards for documents acceptable for entry to the United States. These standards are highest for VWP travelers. For example, the electronic passports mandated by the VWP enable DHS to incorporate biometric verification—digital photographs and, increasingly, fingerprints—in the screening process to confirm that the person presenting the document is the person that the document describes. And, DHS routinely audits the document production and issuance process in VWP countries to ensure standards are being met. In other words, VWP makes it harder to enter the United States using fraudulent documents and forged identities.

These three elements—who's risky, who's coming here, and who's who—work together both prior to take-off and at the port of entry to help U.S. officials identify terrorists and criminals and prevent them from traveling here.

STRENGTHENING THE VWP

It is essential that we continually look to identify possible enhancements to the VWP in the face of current threats, much like DHS continually evaluates participating countries and recommends improvements to their security postures. In addition to program suspension authority, the Visa Waiver Program Improvement Act of 2015 proposes other sensible ways to strengthen the program and build on its successes, such as requiring an evaluation of ESTA and making a handful of discretionary considerations mandatory. However, any measure that would curtail the program even temporarily would be damaging and wrongheaded. Rather than enhance U.S. security, such a step would undermine it, resulting in the loss of significant leverage over the security standards of both current and prospective members, to say nothing of the severe economic and diplomatic consequences.

For current VWP members, suspension of the program would undermine current information and intelligence-sharing mechanisms and deprive the United States of visibility into their security practices, including those to prevent radicalization and identify and track foreign fighters. It would also undermine relationships with our closest allies in the face of common threats ranging from ISIS to a resurgent Russia. For prospective members, the disappearance of the program would remove a powerful and proven incentive to elevate security standards and to enhance cooperation with the United States on security matters.

While emotional responses often occur in times of heightened security concerns, any discussion of the VWP and U.S. security must remain focused on the facts. And the facts are that the VWP has proven to be an effective leverage point for raising and maintaining security standards while providing unprecedented levels of information sharing and access, allowing the United States to better manage risk. To return to the question posed in the hearing's title, the Visa Waiver Program undoubtedly has helped to keep our Nation safe. Implementing sensible enhancements, such as those proposed by H.R. 158, can ensure that it will continue to do so.

Again, thank you for inviting me to testify today. I look forward to answering any questions the subcommittee may have.

Mrs. MILLER. Thank you.

The Chairman now recognizes Mr. Dow for his testimony.

STATEMENT OF ROGER J. DOW, PRESIDENT AND CHIEF EXECUTIVE OFFICER, U.S. TRAVEL ASSOCIATION

Mr. DOW. Thank you. That is very nice of you. Thank you.

The travel industry's top priority is ensuring that travelers are safe and secure. Without security, there is no travel. If travelers don't feel safe, they will stay home. The economic benefits of travel are well-documented. Since submitting my written testimony, I have now received the numbers for 2014. Direct travel spending in the United States was $927 billion. That generated $2.1 trillion in economic output and more than $141 million in tax revenue. Travel directly employed 8 million Americans is and a top-10 employer in 49 States and the District of Columbia.

In-bound long-haul or overseas international travel is an extremely lucrative segment for the United States. The Visa Waiver Program is the largest source of overseas visitors—20.3 million, or 60 percent, of all overseas visitors arrived through the Visa Waiver Program in 2014. Last year, they generated $190 billion in economic output and supported nearly 1 million good American jobs.

Expansion of the Visa Waiver Program has yielded substantial economic benefit. Following the recent admissions of Taiwan and Chile, travel from there rose sharply. This is no surprise, given the staggering increase of visitors from South Korea since its inclusion in 2008. In 2014, a record number of South Korean visitors, 1.5 million, visited the United States, which is a 91 percent increase since they entered the program. They spend $5.1 billion, which is 64 percent higher than 2008, and supported 43,000 good American jobs. Travel is the largest export now from South Korea, constituting 11 percent of the total exports to that country.

When countries enter the Visa Waiver Program, they add billions of dollars to the economy and tens of thousands of good American jobs. Speaking of jobs, the travel industry was hit hard by the economic downturn. But we are a very resilient industry. We helped lead the recovery by expanding employment 36 percent faster than the rest of the economy. Largely as a result of the Visa Waiver Program, travel is our Nation's No. 1 services export, generating $76 billion in 2014.

While these economic figures are very positive, they only tell half the story. International travel is equally critical to our National security. Through travel, we foster closer relationships with visitors that protect us over the long term. Simply said, the more they know us, the more they like us. Beyond public diplomacy, the protocols demanded by the—mandated by the Visa Waiver Program has significantly enhanced our National security, particularly since Congress amended the program in 2007.

Visa Waiver partner nations, while they are strong allies, must still meet rigorous counterterrorism, border security, aviation security, and document security standards, as well as participate, as has just been said, in intelligence and information-sharing arrangements with the United States. Visa Waiver countries must also issue ICAO-compliant electronic passports to their citizens and report all lost and stolen passports immediately to the United States through Interpol. Plus, each Visa Waiver traveler must obtain permission to board a flight to the United States through the electronic system of travel authorization.

Finally, the Visa Waiver Program provides the U.S. Government with the authority to regularly audit, just as my colleague has said. The Visa Waiver Program enables us to better detect, apprehend, and limit the movement of terrorists, criminals, and other dangerous travelers, and to shift the limited visa screening resources we have to higher-risk countries. That is why National security experts across the political spectrum, including every Secretary of

Homeland Security, agree; the Visa Waiver Program is essential and an essential secure tool.

While the Visa Waiver Program helps keep us safer, we should never stop improving it. We believe that any changes should first elevate security, be based on fact not hearsay, minimize disruption of legitimate travelers. That is why U.S. Travel supports H.R. 158. It would upgrade threat assessment and explicitly define the U.S. authority to suspend or revoke Visa Waiver status.

By contrast, proposals to terminate or suspend the Visa Waiver Program would do incalculable harm to both the National and economic security. It would cause mayhem to the visa process that would have to take up all the slack and result in reciprocity against Americans who want to travel abroad. In fact, to improve security, we should expand the Visa Waiver Program, not curtail it, as representatives Joe Heck and Mike Quigley have proposed.

For U.S. Travel, nothing matters more than the safety of our Nation and our travelers. We appreciate your holding this hearing to explore how the Visa Waiver Program protects our homeland while facilitating trade and travel and how the Visa Waiver Program can perform both these twin missions even better. Thank you.

[The prepared statement of Mr. Dow follows:]

PREPARED STATEMENT OF ROGER J. DOW

MARCH 17, 2015

Chairman Miller, Ranking Member Vela, and Members of the subcommittee: I am pleased to offer testimony on behalf of the U.S. Travel Association (U.S. Travel), the National non-profit organization representing all sectors of America's travel community.

I've testified numerous times over the years on the economic impact of travel and tourism and the critical importance of promoting travel and trade. Typically I have been asked to document the significance of the Visa Waiver Program (VWP) to America's economic competitiveness. Overall, the evidence is clear: The Visa Waiver Program is essential to the economic security of the United States.

Today, after briefly reviewing that evidence, I'd also like to focus on the travel industry's top priority: Ensuring that travelers are safe and secure. Without security there is no travel. If travelers don't feel safe, they stay home.

The travel community supports travel policies and programs—like the VWP—that ensure a strong and secure Nation, supported by a resilient and robust economy. We also support continuous oversight of these programs, as the subcommittee is conducting today—and if needed, effective reforms, such as those proposed in H.R. 158, the Visa Waiver Improvement Act and in the JOLT Act.

And if at all possible, we support changing the name of the program. Half of its problem is that the phrase "visa waiver" makes it sound like security is short-changed—when the truth is that the program significantly enhances National security.

TRAVEL AND ECONOMIC SECURITY

It is difficult to overstate the benefits of travel, especially international travel, to the economic security of the United States. In all 50 States, travel provides good domestic jobs that cannot be outsourced. In 2013, direct travel spending in the United States totaled $888 billion, which generated a total of $2.1 trillion in economic output and more than $134 billion in tax revenue. Travel also directly employed 7.9 million Americans and was among the top 10 employers in 49 U.S. States and the District of Columbia. In every region of America, travel expenditures and the taxes they generate help pay the salaries of police, firefighters, and teachers without creating much new demand for those public services.

The most lucrative segment of this sector is "long-haul" or overseas travel to the United States. The overseas traveler stays longer and spends more while here—an average of 17.5 nights and nearly $4,700 per trip. For every 34 overseas travelers who decide to visit the United States, an additional American job is created. The

VWP is the largest source of in-bound overseas travel to the United States providing reciprocal 90-day, visa-free travel for citizens of the 38 countries that currently qualify. More than 19.5 million travelers, 61 percent of all overseas visitors to the United States, arrived in 2013 through the VWP. While here, they generated $190 billion in economic output for the U.S. economy and supported nearly 1 million jobs. Largely as a result of the VWP, travel is our Nation's No. 1 services export, generating a trade surplus of $75.6 billion in 2014.

Recent rounds of VWP expansion have demonstrated substantial economic benefits. Following the recent admissions of Taiwan and Chile, travel demand rose sharply. This is no surprise, given the example of the staggering increase in visitors from South Korea since its inclusion in VWP in late 2008. In 2013, a record 1.4 million visitors from South Korea arrived in the United States, growing by 79 percent since 2008. In 2013, South Korean visitors spent $4.5 billion while traveling in the United States—52 percent higher than in 2008—and supported 39,000 American jobs. Travel (including education/health care-related travel) is now the largest U.S. industry export to South Korea, constituting 11 percent of total U.S. exports of goods and services to South Korea.

The travel industry was not spared by the economic downturn, but we are a resilient industry. From 2010 to the end of 2014, we have added 833,000 jobs, restoring employment to pre-recession levels. We helped lead the recovery by expanding employment at a 36 percent faster pace than the rest of the economy. And these are jobs with significant opportunity for upward mobility, compounding the benefits of this surge in job growth over time.

Finally, while the word "travel" frequently connotes tourism, business travel accounts for 30 percent of all travel spending. In 2013, business travel generated an estimated $267 billion in direct spending—3 percent higher than the previous year. Totaling the deals done, products sold and opportunities created at industry conferences and trade shows, business travel directly supports 2.3 million American workers.

In addition, at a time when Congress and the Obama administration are considering an important trade agenda with Europe and Asia, ensuring smooth movement of business travelers will ensure that visa barriers do not undermine the full benefits of trade liberalization. A study conducted in 2010 by Oxford Economics found that foreign exhibition and buyers spent on average, more than $36,100 each and $13,600 each, respectively while attending U.S. exhibitions.

TRAVEL AND NATIONAL SECURITY

These economic figures—as positive as they are—only tell half of the travel story. International travel is equally critical to our National security. Through travel, we forge new or strengthen existing relationships and alliances and we foster a common understanding that protects our long-term interests. The most effective ambassadors of American values are ordinary Americans. Overseas travelers form life-long impressions of American society based on their visits to destinations, large and small, across America. From our National parks to our ballparks to our theme parks, the heartland of our great Nation reflects the best of the United States to foreign visitors. The more they know us, the better they like us.

Surveys have shown that foreigners who have the opportunity to visit the United States are 74 percent more likely to have a favorable view of our country; and that 61 percent are more likely to support the United States and its policies. Travel has demonstrated significant public diplomacy value as a "soft power" tool that complements our formal foreign policy mechanisms.

By strengthening our alliances and enhancing our Nation's global image, travel has helped to keep us safer. Travel programs can also contribute directly to our National security. The VWP provides an excellent illustration. Since its creation in the 1980s, the Visa Waiver Program has evolved into an invaluable instrument of U.S. National security and public diplomacy. In particular, Congress re-shaped the VWP in 2007 so that it significantly enhances U.S. counterterrorism efforts and strengthens international partnerships.

VWP partner nations are, by definition, strong security allies who meet rigorous conditions in order to be part of the program. For example, VWP countries must meet strict counter-terrorism, border security, aviation security, and document security standards, as well as participate in intelligence- and information-sharing arrangements with the United States. VWP countries must issue International Civil Aviation Organization-compliant electronic passports to their citizens and report information on all lost and stolen passports to the United States through INTERPOL. In addition, each VWP traveler must also obtain permission to board a flight to the United States through the Electronic System for Travel Authorization (ESTA). Finally, the VWP provides the U.S. Government the ability to regularly audit these security requirements to ensure compliance. In short, the VWP enables us to better detect, apprehend, and limit the movement of terrorists, criminals, and other dangerous travelers—and to shift limited visa screening resources to higher-risk countries.

National security experts from across the political spectrum agree that the VWP is a tried and tested security tool. The last three Secretaries of Homeland Security have praised the program's contribution to U.S. and international security. Former Secretary Chertoff recently captured this consensus stating, "I think the Visa Waiver Program is a plus-plus for our National security and for our economic security. I think that we have constructed a program that makes a reduction in vulnerabilities very powerful."

Travel is a perception business where facts can often be distorted by fear and rumor. In the context of the recent terrorist attacks in France, a Visa Waiver Program nation, some mistakenly believe that bad actors could use VWP to board planes to the United States without thorough security checks. The travel industry is committed to educating stakeholders—including Congress—about the fundamental security rationale for the VWP. It is imperative that policymakers and the public understand the current security protocols within VWP and how the program is part of a layered approach to protect the United States and the traveling public.

Along those lines, it is very important to remember that over the past decade, the United States has constructed a significant new capability to screen all travelers, whether they hold a visa, are traveling under the VWP, or are returning U.S. citizens, against up-to-date watch lists. This real-time check allows law enforcement to utilize the most recent intelligence prior to boarding an international flight, and is a critical layer in securing travel, no matter how a traveler was originally authorized to travel to the United States.

THE FUTURE OF THE VWP

We should never stop assessing and improving the programs that safeguard National security. While we believe the VWP helps to keep us safer, U.S. Travel can support sensible reforms that further buttress security. In our view, any such changes should:
- Offer elevated levels of personal and National security while;
- Focusing on areas of concern that are based on fact, not merely hearsay; and
- To the extent possible, minimizing disruption to legitimate travelers.

The proposals contained in H.R. 158 meet these criteria. The bill would significantly upgrade reporting on potential visitors from overseas, threat assessments; and explicitly define U.S. authority to suspend or revoke a country's VWP status. Accordingly, the travel industry supports this legislation—and stands ready to work with you to see it enacted into law.

U.S. Travel also believes it is important for our National and economic security, to expand the VWP to a select group of countries. For precisely that reason, U.S. Travel also supports the JOLT Act, legislation introduced by Representatives Joe Heck and Mike Quigley that would add more layers of security while also giving the Secretary of Homeland Security greater flexibility to expand the program to countries that meet the appropriate security criteria.

By contrast, proposals to terminate or suspend the VWP would do incalculable harm to both our National and economic security. Shutting down programs like the VWP that not only facilitate travel but also provide valuable information to our counterterrorism and law enforcement officials is not a formula to keeping us safe. Lastly, any rollback of visa waiver privileges will cause the partner country to reinstate visa requirements for U.S. citizens traveling abroad, to their inconvenience and to the detriment of international trade.

It is the incentive to participate in the VWP that has pushed all 38 VWP to improve their security posture. A number of countries, for example, have unilaterally upgraded their passports so as to be eligible for the VWP. Likewise, several prospective members have signed the information-sharing agreements and otherwise increased law enforcement and security-related cooperation with the United States in the hopes of meeting the program's requirements. These actions provide tangible security benefits to the United States and to the international traveling public.

For U.S. Travel, nothing matters more than the safety of our Nation and travelers. We appreciate your holding this hearing to explore how the Visa Waiver Program advances the critical mission of protecting our homeland while also facilitating trade and travel—and how VWP could perform that mission even better.

Again, thank you Chairman Miller, Ranking Member Vela, and all Members of the subcommittee for inviting me to testify today. I look forward to answering your questions.

Mrs. MILLER. Thank you very much, Mr. Dow. The Chairman now recognizes Dr. Bucci for his testimony.

STATEMENT OF STEVEN P. BUCCI, DIRECTOR, THE DOUGLAS AND SARAH ALLISON CENTER FOR FOREIGN AND NATIONAL SECURITY POLICY, THE HERITAGE FOUNDATION

Mr. BUCCI. Madam Chairman, Members, my name is Steven Bucci. I am the director of the Allison Center at Heritage. The views I express in this testimony are my own and should not be construed as representing any official position of the Heritage Foundation.

I spent a majority of my life in the military. I retired as an Army colonel, having served as a defense attaché in several embassies and having served as a commander in special forces fighting terrorism. I also served as the deputy assistant secretary of defense for homeland defense for several years.

I will focus on two aspects of the VWP; the security and foreign policy pieces. News of European passport holders joining ISIS created concern about radicalized Western fighters abusing the program to engage in terrorism. This is a poor reason to scale back or end this program. The VWP promotes security. The ISIS threat only emphasizes the importance of its intel-sharing requirements.

Currently, the nations participating are required to share intelligence about known or suspected terrorists, exchange biographic, biometric, and criminal data, share information on lost and stolen passports, increase airport security, and provide reciprocal travel without a visa.

I have included a graphic in my written testimony. It shows side-by-side the ways a VWP traveler interfaces with the U.S. Government systems and the way a non-VWP traveler does. The bottom line is there are only two steps that are differences of note, two things that are skipped by a VWP traveler. The first is the face-to-face interview with Consular Services. The second is the pre-travel input of biometric data.

While I am not here to criticize the fine young folks who work at the consular desks in our embassies, but I have been there in several of them. About 25 percent of those face-to-face interviews are done by first-tour foreign service officers right out of training. They are not intel or law enforcement experts. The remaining 75 percent of the face-to-face interviews are done by foreign service nationals, local hires under the general supervision of our consular personnel.

In the VWP, we lose that step. But in return, we get the enhanced information sharing with the host nation law enforcement and intel services and access to their databases of potentially dangerous persons. As a former HUMINT collector and Green Beret, I am pretty comfortable saying that we get a lot more protection and security from that info sharing than we do from those face-to-face interviews, an incomparably greater amount of protection and security.

The second skipped step, frankly, is also a wash. We lose the pre-travel biometric input. But in return, as mentioned, all the VWP travelers have to travel with a machine-readable, biometrically-tagged passport, which is checked at their arrival point so we basically make up for that lost step. In short, the VWP gives us better security, not less.

With regard to foreign policy, we have treaty allies right who are not allowed into the VWP because they have not reached the 3 percent or less visa refusal rate and DHS no longer has the authority to waive it up to 10 percent. This is mistake. Given the many benefits of the VWP, the United States should be examining how to increase the membership judiciously. DHS should be allowed to waive the 3 percent limit, and Congress should add a low visa overstay rate, a better metric, which uses the country's overstay rates as a measure of how their citizens respect the terms of their entry into the United States.

While such permanent reform would be ideal, Congress could at least seek to return the waiver authority to DHS on a short-term or one-time basis, allowing the Secretary to accept treaty allies such as Poland into the VWP as long as their visa refusal rate were below that 10 percent mark. Such an action would help the United States economically, improve security, and remind our allies, especially those like Poland that face an ever-more aggressive Russia, that the United States stands with them.

The administration should be asked to provide the committee a list of countries that are in that category and whose general behavior and cooperation warranted for inclusion in the VWP. It should be done quickly and should be heralded as just what it is; a reward for positive behavior. But it is a reward that also benefits the United States greatly. Thank you.

[The prepared statement of Mr. Bucci follows:]

PREPARED STATEMENT OF STEVEN P. BUCCI

MARCH 17, 2015

My name is Steven Bucci. I am director of the Douglas and Sarah Allison Center for Foreign and National Security Policy in The Heritage Foundation's Davis Institute for National Security and Foreign Policy. The views I express in this testimony are my own, and should not be construed as representing any official position of The Heritage Foundation.

I have spent the majority of my life as a military officer; I retired from the Army as a colonel, having served as a defense attaché, a human intelligence collector working in embassies for Defense Intelligence Agency (DIA), and as a Special Forces operator and commander of the 3d Battalion, 5th Special Forces Group, fighting terrorism. I also served as the deputy assistant secretary of defense for homeland defense, DOD's representative to the Interagency for Counter Terrorism domestically.

VWP AND THE THREAT OF TERROR

The Visa Waiver Program (VWP) is a valuable tool supporting U.S. tourism and trade, public diplomacy, and National security. The VWP allows residents of member countries to visit the United States without a visa for up to 90 days in exchange for security-cooperation and information-sharing arrangements and reciprocal travel privileges for U.S. residents.

News of European passport holders joining the Islamic State in Iraq and al Sham (ISIS), however, have created concerns about radicalized Western fighters abusing the VWP to engage in terrorism here in the United States. These concerns, however, are not a good reason to end the VWP. The VWP promotes security and the ISIS threat only emphasizes the importance of the VWP's intelligence-sharing requirements and adding appropriate nations to the program.

18

In order to become a VWP member, a country must:
- Demonstrate a non-immigrant-visa refusal rate (the percentage of visa applicants denied by the State Department for a particular nation) of no more than 3 percent;
- Issue all its residents secure, machine-readable biometric passports; and
- Present no discernable threat to U.S. law enforcement or U.S. National security.

Currently, 38 nations are participating in the VWP.[1] As required by the VWP and certain laws, these nations have also agreed to various stipulations and obligations, including requirements to:
- Share intelligence about known or suspected terrorists with the United States (per Homeland Security Presidential Directive 6 (HSPD–6));
- Exchange biographic, biometric, and criminal data with the United States (automated, via Preventing and Combating Serious Crime (PCSC) agreements);
- Share information on lost and stolen passports (LASP agreements);
- Increase their own airport security requirements; and
- Provide U.S. citizens with a reciprocal ability to travel to that country without a visa.[2]

These features greatly enhance security by providing U.S. law enforcement and security agencies with more information and intelligence on potential terrorists and other bad actors. The VWP makes it easier for U.S. officials to know whether an individual presents a security threat. The VWP also allows the State Department to focus its consular and visa resources on those countries and individuals about which less is known and are higher risks to U.S. security.

Furthermore, the VWP includes robust screening and security procedures. Every traveler to the United States from a VWP country must be pre-screened through the Electronic System for Travel Authorization (ESTA). ESTA data is then checked against multiple databases including Custom and Border Protection's (CBP) Automating Targeting System (ATS) and TECS system. The ATS is run by the National Targeting Center and checks a variety of databases including the Terrorist Screening Database (TSDB) and Interpol's data on lost and stolen passports. The ATS gives each individual a risk-based score that determines whether or not the individual should receive additional scrutiny or inspection. TECS queries various databases for information about the person's eligibility for travel to the United States and whether he or she is a known security risk.[3] TECS also checks against the TSDB, which is maintained by the FBI for law enforcement use in apprehending or stopping known or suspected terrorists.[4]

Additionally, when individuals buy their tickets, that information is forwarded from the airlines to the Department of Homeland Security (DHS) and checked through multiple systems. The Transportation Security Administration's Secure Flight program collects passenger data and compares it against the TSDB's No-Fly and Selectee lists. CBP's Advance Passenger Information System (APIS) collects the Passenger Name Record and other information about travelers and forwards the information to the Arrival and Departure Information System (ADIS) to help combat visa overstays, and also to the National Targeting Center and the ATS to detect high-risk travelers.[5]

---

[1] U.S. Department of State, Bureau of Consular Affairs, "U.S. Visas: Visa Waiver Program," *http://travel.state.gov/content/visas/english/visit/visa-waiver-program.html* (accessed March 12, 2015).

[2] Alison Siskin, "Visa Waiver Program," Congressional Research Service *Report for Congress*, February 12, 2014, *http://fas.org/sgp/crs/homesec/RL32221.pdf* (accessed March 12, 2015).

[3] Lisa Seghetti, "Border Security: Immigration Inspections at Ports of Entry," Congressional Research Service *Report for Congress*, January 26, 2015, pp. 9–10, *http://fas.org/sgp/crs/homesec/R43356.pdf* (accessed March 12, 2015).

[4] Timothy J. Healy, "Statement Before the House Judiciary Committee," Federal Bureau of Investigation, March 24, 2010, *http://www.fbi.gov/news/testimony/sharing-and-analyzing-information-to-prevent-terrorism* (accessed March 12, 2015).

[5] Seghetti, "Border Security: Immigration Inspections at Ports of Entry."

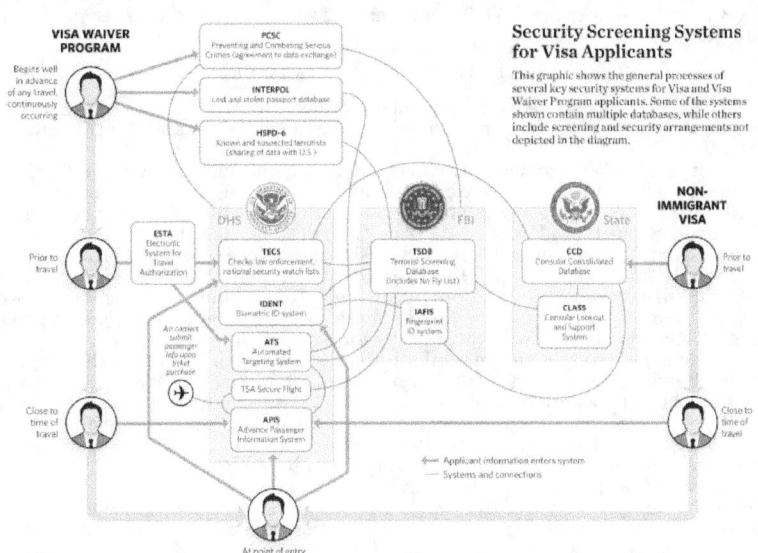

Upon landing in the United States, individuals must provide biographic and biometric information that is checked against additional sets of biometric databases controlled by DHS (Automated Biometric Identification System or IDENT) and the FBI (Integrated Automated Fingerprint Identification System or IAFIS). The individual is once again checked through TECS, the ATS, and the APIS and undergoes additional inspection if necessary. At any point in this process, security officials can prevent an individual from entering the United States if they are deemed a security risk or ineligible for travel to the United States. While no system is without flaws, this is a robust screening process.[6]

The main differences between this screening process and the traditional visa screening process are that a traditional visa applicant must have an in-person interview at a U.S. consulate and provide biometric data prior to obtaining a visa. This allows biometric checks to occur prior to travel. The traditional visa process, however, does not have the same information-sharing arrangements that are required to be a part of the VWP that provide the United States with data on known and suspected terrorists and serious criminals.

Since the VWP was created in 1986, tourism and related expenditures in the United States have dramatically increased. From 2000 to 2013, the number of visitors to the United States increased by 18.6 million, a 36 percent increase, to a record number of 69.8 million, with approximately 40 percent of all visitors entering the United States through the VWP.[7] As a result, the VWP has helped the United States maintain a trade surplus in tourism since 1989, with visitors spending $180.7 billion in 2013, supporting the travel and tourism industries that constitute 2.8 percent of U.S. gross domestic product, including 8 million jobs, as well as many other sectors of the U.S. economy, such as restaurant and consumer-good businesses.[8]

The VWP is also an important tool of foreign policy and public diplomacy. Allowing individuals to visit the United States and enjoy our country can improve the foreign public's understanding and appreciation for America and our culture. By extending the privilege of the VWP to other nations, we deepen diplomatic ties with friendly governments and allies, as well. A graphic depiction of these processes is

[6] Ibid., pp. 10–11.

[7] Siskin, "Visa Waiver Program," and U.S. Department of Commerce, Office of Travel and Tourism Industries, "International Arrivals to U.S. by Region and Country of Residency: Historical Visitation 2000–2006," *http://travel.trade.gov/outreachpages/download__data__table/Historical__arrivals__2000__2006.pdf* (accessed March 12, 2015).

[8] International Trade Administration, National Travel and Tourism Office, "Fast Facts: United States Travel and Tourism Industry 2013," *http://travel.trade.gov/outreachpages/download__data__table/Fast__Facts__2013.pdf* (accessed March, 2015).

attached to this submission, showing a side-by-side comparison of the interaction of a VWP traveler and a non-VWP traditional traveler with the various parts of the U.S. systems.

IMPROVEMENT AND EXPANSION

While the VWP boosts security, diplomacy, trade, and tourism, there are areas for improvement, including information-sharing arrangements and metrics for visa overstays.

As mentioned, VWP participants must enter into various information-sharing arrangements with the United States, as mandated by the 9/11 Commission Act of 2007. In 2012, the U.S. Government Accountability Office's (GAO's) Acting Director of Homeland Security and Justice Rebecca Gambler testified that many nations had not finalized these agreements or begun sharing information. According to GAO data as of January 2011, only 19 of the 36 VWP nations had agreed to share terrorist-watch-list information and only 13 were actually sharing information. Worse yet, only 18 of 36 nations had agreed to share PCSC crime information, and no information-sharing arrangements were fully automated as required.[9]

Since then, however, action on information sharing has dramatically improved: The Congressional Research Service reported that nearly all VWP members had agreed to share information as of February 2014,[10] and, according to a DHS legislative affairs official, as of September 2014 all nations are now sharing information on terrorists, serious criminals, and lost or stolen passports. DHS is, however, still working to automate PCSC data sharing for all VWP participants.[11] Congress should ensure that progress on these agreements continues.

Given the many benefits of the VWP, the United States should also examine how to increase VWP membership judiciously. The requirement for a biometric visa-exit system, which is not a cost-effective tool for stopping terrorism or illegal immigration, currently stands in the way of most nations joining the VWP.[12] DHS should be allowed to waive the 3 percent limit on non-immigrant visa-refusal rates, and Congress should add a requirement for low visa-overstay rates instead. The visa-refusal metric is susceptible to subjective decisions by different visa consular officers in different countries that can affect the number of visas refused and granted. A better metric would be to use countries' visa-overstay rates as a measure of how a country's citizens respect the terms of their entry into, and time in, the United States. While such reform would be ideal and more permanent, Congress could also seek to return waiver authority to the DHS Secretary on a short-term basis, allowing the Secretary to accept treaty allies such as Poland into the VWP, so long as their visa-refusal rate was less than 10 percent. Such action would help the United States economically, improve security and screening of individuals coming to the United States, and would remind our allies, especially those like Poland that face an increasingly aggressive Russia, that the United States stands by them.

Additional measures, to strengthen the ESTA application or to provide DHS with reasonable tools to ensure member countries are abiding by their agreements, could also be worthwhile reforms. Countries that do not meet the terms of the VWP should face consequences, but full expulsion from the program should not be used lightly.

CONCLUSION

With many benefits, the VWP is more valuable than ever. The threat of ISIS and radicalized Westerners is real and the United States should be using all the intelligence tools at its disposal to find and stop these terrorists. The VWP is one of those tools, and to stop it now would make the United States less secure, less pros-

[9] Rebecca Gambler, "Visa Waiver Program: Additional Actions Needed to Mitigate Risks and Strengthen Overstay Enforcement," Government Accountability Office, GAO–12–599T, March 27, 2012, *http://www.gao.gov/assets/590/589621.pdf* (accessed March 12, 2015), and Jessica Zuckerman, "The Visa Waiver Program: Time for Nations to Bear the Consequences of Non-Compliance," Heritage Foundation *Issue Brief* No. 3565, April 12, 2012, *http://www.heritage.org/research/reports/2012/04/visawaiver-program-consequences-of-non-compliance.*

[10] Siskin, "Visa Waiver Program."

[11] Gambler, "Visa Waiver Program," and phone conversation between David Inserra and DHS official, DHS Office of Legislative Affairs, September 10, 2014.

[12] Steven P. Bucci and David Inserra, "Biometric Exit Improvement Act: Wrong Solution to Broken Visa and Immigration System," Heritage Foundation *Issue Brief* No. 4064, October 8, 2013, *http://www.heritage.org/research/reports/2013/10/biometric-exit-improvement-act-and-the-broken-visa-and-immigration-system,* and Jessica Zuckerman, "Taiwan Admitted to the Visa Waiver Program," Heritage Foundation *Issue Brief* No. 3747, October 3, 2012, *http://www.heritage.org/research/reports/2012/10/taiwan-admitted-to-the-visa-waiver-program.*

perous, and less engaged with friends and allies. Instead, we should be looking to improve and expand the program.

Mrs. MILLER. Thank you very much, Doctor.

The Chairman now recognizes Mr. Jenkins.

STATEMENT OF BRIAN MICHAEL JENKINS, SENIOR ADVISER TO THE RAND PRESIDENT, THE RAND CORPORATION

Mr. JENKINS. Chairman Miller, Ranking Member Vela, and distinguished Members of the committee, thank you very much for the opportunity to address this important subject.

The testimony I have already submitted addresses two fundamental questions. One is the threat posed by Western fighters who have joined Jihadist fronts in Syria and Iran. No. 2, how can the United States enhance its ability to identify and intercept returning foreign fighters with passports from countries currently covered by the Visa Waiver Program?

You know, one of the advantages of going fourth here is that you can revise your order of remarks along the way. What I am about to do is just toss my oral remarks completely. Let me just underscore a few points that have already being touched upon.

First of all, the threat. This is serious. The continuing civil war in Syria, ISIL's military victories, and its claimed re-creation of the caliphate has created a great deal of excitement and has attracted foreign fighters from around the world. The numbers are constantly on the move. But we are looking at in excess of 20,000 foreign fighters who have now gone to Syria. Most of these are from Arab countries, but more than 3,000 are from Western countries, primarily Europe.

The bombing campaign by the coalition does not appear to have stopped this flow yet. In fact, just last week the Prime Minister of France said that they could expect 10,000 European fighters in Syria and Iraq by the end of this year. That is—now, this is a dangerous bunch. I mean, ISIL recruits people who are not simply—not only not repelled by images of beheadings and burning people alive and crucifixions and mass executions, that is its recruiting poster. It is gathering, assembling people who are looking for opportunities to participate in that.

Its al-Qaeda counterpart remains dedicated to attacking the far enemy; that is us. Right now, ISIL is not so concerned with launching attacks abroad. But under pressure, that strategy could change. If ISIL is defeated, then we could see the proliferation of small groups on the run bent upon revenge. So the threat is serious.

Visa Waiver Program. Look, our allies here understand they have got a major problem in Europe. The recent terrorist attacks underscore that. So they are taking a number of steps now to improve intelligence, to increase their criminal penalties. This allows us some real opportunities to work with them. One of the things that they are doing, for example, is adding elements to the PNR. We can use that information if it is shared with us in conjunction with the information that we get through ESTA in order to create new kinds of profiles that will identify these people coming in.

We are gonna have to shift our thinking here. The problem was overstay. The issue now is intercept. So the challenge for us is how we can take things like ESTA, PNR data, intelligence data, prescreening processes which are being extended abroad, as well as arrival procedures by customs and immigration officials, and knit them together into a National strategy.

So the point is this isn't just about Visa Waiver. Visa Waiver is a component of a larger necessary effort which is gonna have to go on for a long time because we are going to be dealing with the effluent of the fighting in Syria and Iraq for the foreseeable future. Thank you.

[The prepared statement of Mr. Jenkins follows:]

PREPARED STATEMENT OF BRIAN MICHAEL JENKINS [1]

MARCH 17, 2015

CONTAINING MIDDLE EAST TERROR MEASURES TO REDUCE THE THREAT POSED BY FOREIGN FIGHTERS RETURNING FROM SYRIA AND IRAQ [2]

Chairman Miller, Ranking Member Vela, distinguished Members of the subcommittee, I would like to thank you for the opportunity to address this important subject.

My testimony will address two fundamental questions:

(1) What is the threat posed by Western fighters who have joined jihadist fronts in Syria and Iraq?

(2) How can the United States enhance its ability to identify and intercept returning foreign fighters with passports from European and other countries that are currently covered by the Visa Waiver Program?

Let's begin with the threat.

Over the past 8 months, my colleagues at RAND have had several opportunities to offer Congressional committees their assessments of the evolving threat posed by jihadist groups in the Middle East and North Africa. [3] While the focus of my colleagues and their interpretations of the evolving threat vary, I regard my own testimony to be the latest installment this continuing body of work. [4]

Syria's civil war, Assad's brutal repression, the spread of jihadist ideology, the growing sectarianism of the conflict in Syria and Iraq, the military victories achieved by the Islamic State of Iraq and the Levant (ISIL), and, perhaps above all, ISIL's announced re-creation of the Caliphate have galvanized would-be jihadist warriors throughout the world.

According to the latest reported intelligence estimate, 20,000 foreign fighters have traveled from other countries to join the fight in Syria and Iraq. [5] Most are believed to have joined ISIL. "Estimate" is the operative word here, but if the number is close to correct, this would mean that foreign fighters now comprise a large portion of ISIL's total strength—estimated to be as many as 31,000 fighters—and enough to influence its trajectory. Most of the volunteers come from other Arab countries, but the National Counterterrorism Center (NCTC) has estimated 3,400 have come

---

[1] The opinions and conclusions expressed in this testimony are the author's alone and should not be interpreted as representing those of RAND or any of the sponsors of its research. This product is part of the RAND Corporation testimony series. RAND testimonies record testimony presented by RAND associates to Federal, State, or local legislative committees; Government-appointed commissions and panels; and private review and oversight bodies. The RAND Corporation is a nonprofit research organization providing objective analysis and effective solutions that address the challenges facing the public and private sectors around the world. RAND's publications do not necessarily reflect the opinions of its research clients and sponsors.

[2] This testimony is available for free download at *http://www.rand.org/pubs/testimonies/CT427.html*.

[3] See Seth Jones, *Jihadist Sanctuaries in Syria and Iraq: Implications for the United States*, testimony presented before the House Homeland Security Committee, Subcommittee on Counterterrorism and Intelligence on July 24, 2014; Ben Connable, *Defeating the Islamic State in Iraq*, testimony presented before the Senate Foreign Relations Committee on September 17, 2014; and Rick Brennan Jr., *The Growing Strategic Threat of Radical Islamist Ideology*, testimony presented before the House Foreign Affairs Committee on February 12, 2015.

[4] This testimony also builds on my recent previous research, as reported in *The Dynamics of Syria's Civil War*, Santa Monica, Calif.: RAND Corporation, 2014; *Brothers Killing Brothers: The Current Infighting Will Test al Qaeda's Brand*, Santa Monica, Calif.: RAND Corporation, 2014; and *When Jihadis Come Marching Home: The Terrorist Threat Posed by Westerners Returning from Syria and Iraq*, Santa Monica, Calif.: RAND Corporation, 2014.

[5] Nicholas J. Rasmussen, Director of the National Counterterrorism Center, *Current Terrorist Threat to the United States*, testimony before the Senate Select Committee on Intelligence, February 12, 2015.

from Europe and other Western countries and are therefore theoretically eligible to enter the United States without a visa. Most of these Western volunteers are believed to have joined ISIL, which now calls itself the Islamic State.

The coalition bombing campaign—which was intended to: (1) Contain ISIL by supporting partners on the ground, such as the Kurdish Peshmerga, who are reclaiming territory lost earlier to ISIL; (2) prevent ISIL from being able to move freely in Syria and Iraq; (3) disrupt and degrade its command and control; (4) reduce its logistical capabilities; and (5) target key leaders where possible—has taken a toll on ISIL's operational capabilities. But it does not appear to have significantly reduced the flow of Western fighters to Syria and Iraq: The reported numbers have continued to increase since the bombing campaign began in September 2014. In part, the growing numbers may reflect a time lag as authorities learn about those who departed before the bombing campaign began. However, there is evidence that the flow of recruits continues. France's prime minister recently forecast that by the end of this year, as many as 10,000 Europeans may join the jihadist front in Syria and Iraq.

ISIL'S RECRUITING ATTRACTS THE VIOLENCE-PRONE

ISIL operates a sophisticated recruiting program, which includes its highly-publicized victories and its equally well-recorded atrocities. Its message is disseminated through its official outlets on the internet and reinforced by a distributed recruiting campaign by its own members using social media. ISIL appeals to potential recruits' sense of religious duty—faith undeniably plays a role in recruitment, even though volunteers may not possess a profound knowledge of Islam. Like all true believers, recruits may be attracted by a simple black-and-white, us-versus-them belief system. Poverty and oppression may explain why people in some countries embrace violent extremism, but it does not explain the flow of Western volunteers. Individual biographies of those who have gone to participate in jihad or have attempted to go suggest a variety of personal motives—alienation, perceived insults, personal crises, dissatisfaction with empty spiritual lives, adolescent rebellion, or other discontentment.

ISIL is a dangerous group. It distinguishes itself from other jihadist groups by continuing to publicize its limitless violence. This attracts a self-selecting assembly of individuals who are not repelled by graphic images of mass executions, beheadings, crucifixions, and burnings and who indeed may be attracted by opportunities to participate in such atrocities. They exult in violence. Gathering as a group in Syria and Iraq, they may reinforce each other's savagery, creating a constituency within ISIL that supports escalating violence.

This dynamic is present in most terrorist groups. For the ideologues who initiate terrorist campaigns, violence is instrumental—a means to achieve an end. Violent campaigns attract others who subscribe to the ideology but actually seek membership in a terrorist group as a source of status. For a third cohort, the prospect of violence is the principal attraction—ideology offers a license to kill.

Over time, the harder members of a group dominate decision making. Their argument is always the same—if the group is not doing well, it must become more ruthless. If the group is doing well, escalation will accelerate progress. Hardliners cannot easily be reined in, even if the leaders want to restrain them. Commanders who counsel moderation risk being branded as traitors and eliminated, or hardliners may break off to form their own groups. This is not to say that we have any evidence at all of attempts by ISIL's leaders to moderate the group's activities; instead, they appear to encourage barbarity. Still, there must be some tension between those who want to build a state and those whose increasing barbarity makes them appear determined to trigger its destruction.

Transgression demonstrates conviction and binds the perpetrator to the cause. ISIL seems determined to separate its fighters from normal society. There are reports that the group forces recruits to commit atrocities to ensure their loyalty and reduce chances that they can ever return home.

The accumulation of atrocity increasingly precludes any resolution other than continuing warfare or death. For the group as well as for the individual, having crossed the line into nihilism, there is no way back.

ISIL'S CALCULATED RUTHLESSNESS—STRATEGIC CALCULATION OR COLLECTIVE MADNESS?

To the outside world, ISIL's escalating murder and destruction is incomprehensible. Rational explanations are required.

We invent strategic calculations (or miscalculations) that make mayhem logical. Analysts posit that ISIL's leaders intend its atrocities to provoke the rage that draws in foreign ground forces, where casualties and captures will erode resolve and impose a time limit on foreign military achievement, will incite responses that divide the coalition, or will precipitate action before ISIL's foes are fully prepared to take it on.

Continuing warfare changes the individual outlooks of those involved. Armed conflict can brutalize its participants. Violence, not just on the battlefield but in executions, torture, and mistreatment of prisoners, hostages, and the civilian population, becomes matter-of-fact. Atrocities become routine. This has effects on the mental condition of both the individual and the collective. A gathering of violent zealots can lead to collective madness in which sadistic cruelty becomes an end in itself, requiring no strategic explanation.

It may be unpleasant to contemplate, but we cannot dismiss the power of belief. ISIL has attracted the most fervent disciples to an extreme (many would say discredited) version of Islam, recruits who believe in the imposition of the cruelest form of Islamic law without compromise. This belief system may include apocalyptic thinking; the idea that escalating violence will hasten the final confrontation between true believers and the forces of evil. There is a fierce debate over whether ISIL represents or perverts Islam, but the fact that ISIL's theological pretensions are widely rejected by Muslim clerics, both militant and centrist, is not the point here. Polling data and a continuing flow of recruits from Europe indicate that ISIL's religiously justified violence resonates with some.

There will be Caligulas. To possess unchallenged power over other human beings, beyond the reach of retribution, immune from any restraining moral authority, allows license and cruelty.

Through its strategy of terror, exaltation of violence as a recruiting theme, attraction to and assembly of the most fervent and most ruthless followers, and deliberate rejection of any constraints, ISIL is creating a dangerous population that cannot be easily pacified or reabsorbed into normal life.

THERE ARE SCENARIOS OF IMMEDIATE CONCERN

A long-term terrorist threat that survives the destruction of ISIL warrants our attention, but there also are several scenarios of immediate concern. These include the following:

- A 9/11-like scenario in which foreign volunteers on their way to the front lines in Syria or Iraq are instead recruited and supported to carry out a major terrorist strike in the United States. This is the 9/11 scenario, where the attackers were on their way to an active combat zone when they were instead diverted to a terrorist mission. It seems unlikely that in today's more vigilant environment, terrorists could mount an operation of that scale without being detected.
- A shoe-bomber or underwear bomber scenario in which a single volunteer is recruited and equipped for a suicide mission. There were reports in 2014 of such plotting by al-Qaeda's Khorasan cell, a group of veterans sent from Afghanistan to Syria to recruit and deploy fighters with Western passports.
- 7/7 scenarios, named after the 2005 bombing of public transport in London, in which Westerners are provided with specialized training and dispatched to the West without further support.
- Low-level attacks carried out based on individual initiative. These could involve returning foreign fighters or home-grown terrorists responding to calls by ISIL or al-Qaeda's affiliates to carry out attacks. These might include active-shooter attacks and hostage situations as we have seen in Ottawa, Paris, Sydney, and Copenhagen.

ISIL IS NOT YET COMMITTED TO ATTACKING WESTERN FOES ON THEIR OWN TERRITORY, BUT ITS CONTAINMENT COULD CHANGE ITS STRATEGY

There is no indication yet that ISIL has initiated a terrorist campaign aimed at directly attacking its Western foes on their own territory. It has taunted and threatened the West in widely-disseminated videos showing gruesome murders of Western nationals. It has called upon its supporters abroad to carry out similar acts of terrorism and has praised those who have done so.

However, unlike al-Qaeda, which continues to follow a strategy of attacking the "far enemy," ISIL appears more focused on the expansion and defense of the territory it controls as the Islamic State. This reflects necessity. With an economy based on plunder and an army of fanatics, it is doubtful that the Islamic State could survive as a normal state within static borders even if its enemies were to allow it to try. It must continue to expand or it will consume itself.

Squeezed by ground offensives supported by foreign airpower, ISIL may at some point alter its strategy and carry out attacks abroad in an effort to break the coalition's political resolve. If ISIL does decide to launch attacks abroad, it will be able to draw upon its substantial financial resources and a deep bench of Western volunteers from among its existing fighters.

The defeat of the Islamic State could turn into a scenario of slaughter, as victims of its cruel occupation and even its one-time Sunni allies turn against it if only to preempt Shi'a retribution. But its destruction could also shatter the enterprise into a host of small, desperate groups, on the run, bent upon revenge.

If the Islamic State is brought down, where will its foreign fighters go? Facing a hostile reception if they had returned home, foreign volunteers who went to Afghanistan to fight Soviet invaders in the 1980s gathered under al-Qaeda's banner. Some ISIL veterans will migrate to other fronts in Afghanistan, where ISIL has already set up shop; to the Caucasus, from which a large number of its foreign fighters, including a number of its commanders, come; or to Libya, where ISIL has found new allies. Some Western volunteers, disillusioned by their experience and with nowhere else to go, will simply want to come home. Others will direct their wrath toward the West.

Most face arrest if they return to their home countries, although European countries are divided on how to deal with returning fighters. Instead of prison, some countries want to offer rehabilitation and reintegration into society, at least to some returnees. It will likely be hard to determine the degree of individual participation in atrocities. Given ISIL's record, "re-humanization" may be a prerequisite to rehabilitation. Clearly, there are some advantages to offering a way back if it requires an open declaration of return and willingness to cooperate with authorities.

But rehabilitation programs have had mixed results, and resources for surveillance are already stretched by the number of people going to or returning from jihadist fronts. Authorities may not have the resources needed to effectively monitor significant numbers of individuals at large. This clearly was France's problem in dealing with the rapid rise in the number of persons going to Syria or contemplating going there. And jihadists have shown remarkable persistence, which means they may have to be monitored in some fashion for years.

I think it is safe to assume that foreign fighters from other countries seeking to enter the United States are more likely to have malevolent intentions than returning Americans. Their capabilities for putting together large-scale terrorist operations here may be limited, but not their intentions. ISIL's fighters have set a new benchmark for brutality. They have rejected all arguments to curb their enthusiasm for bloodshed, whether from Islamic theologians or even al-Qaeda's own leaders.

THE AMERICAN EXPERIENCE

Although the numbers continue to grow, the number of individuals from the United States going to jihadist fronts is, fortunately, not anywhere near the number that have gone from Europe. The most recent estimate puts the total of American volunteers at 150, including those who went for reasons related to the conflict in Syria but not to join jihadist fronts, those who attempted to go and were arrested on the way, and those who have gone and been killed while fighting for ISIL or other jihadist groups.

The historical experience of Americans going to other jihadist fronts (in Afghanistan, Pakistan, Somalia, and Yemen) indicates that, of 124 publicly-identified Americans who went or tried to go abroad to join such fronts between 9/11 and the end of 2014, approximately one-third were arrested on the way. Of those who managed to connect with jihadist groups abroad, 24 were killed (six in suicide bombings), 13 were arrested while abroad, and 13 more are still at large. Of the 35 who returned, 9 were involved in subsequent terrorist plots. Only 3 home-grown jihadist attacks in the United States resulted in fatalities. These were carried out by individuals who are not known to have received any terrorist training abroad.[6] (These figures represent only the publicly-identified would-be jihadists; they do not include the total number of those who reportedly traveled to Syria or Iraq.)

Returning American fighters add a layer of threat, but—given their still-modest numbers—it is a threat that I believe is manageable within existing laws and resources. More-effective leveraging of local police can provide needed reinforcements.[7] As our focus here is on the Visa Waiver Program (VWP), returning Americans are

---

[6] Jenkins, *When Jihadis Come Marching Home.*

[7] Brian Michael Jenkins, Andrew Liepman, and Henry H. Willis, *Identifying Enemies Among Us: Evolving Terrorist Threats and the Continuing Challenges of Domestic Intelligence Collection and Information Sharing*, Santa Monica, Calif.: RAND Corporation, 2014. See also Business Executives for National Security, *Domestic Security: Confronting a Changing Threat to Ensure Public Safety and Civil Liberties*, Washington, DC, 2015.

a separate problem. Nevertheless, dealing with that problem should be viewed as part of an overall strategy.

THERE ARE SEVERAL U.S. LINES OF DEFENSE

There are several potential lines of defense, each of which offers opportunities to identify and intercept foreign fighters before they are able to carry out acts of terrorism in the United States.

1. The first line of defense consists of all international efforts to reduce the number of volunteers going to jihadist fronts. While such efforts depend nearly entirely on foreign actions, the United States can nonetheless encourage and support them.

2. The United States could push for broader international efforts to intercept returning fighters, primarily efforts by Turkey and the European Union—especially front-line countries, such as Bulgaria and Greece, whose land borders returning fighters may try to cross. However, foreign fighters may deliberately take roundabout routes to evade detection. Right now, Turkey, as the entry and exit point for virtually all foreign fighters, is key to stemming the flow.

3. Intelligence sources may identify groups engaged in planning terrorist attacks against the West and disrupt their activities or specific plots while the would-be attackers are still abroad. The U.S. bombing of suspected Khorasan cells in Syria is an example of such an effort.

4. The Terrorist Identities Datamart Environment (TIDE), No-Fly List, and other databases derived from intelligence sources are currently the primary mechanism for identifying returning foreign fighters. The question is how much they could be improved by better sharing arrangements with foreign partners in VWP countries.
Intelligence-sharing arrangements are complicated and beyond the scope of my testimony. An agreement is in place that allows E.U. countries to share Passenger Name Record (PNR) information with the United States. In the wake of the recent terrorist attacks in Paris, E.U. interior ministers have proposed a Europe-wide plan that would require passengers to provide additional information, which would remain available to terrorism-related investigations for up to 5 years. The collection and sharing of additional data would provide additional confidence that authorities in the European Union and the United States will be able to accurately identify returning fighters. There is, however, strong opposition from civil libertarians. Meanwhile, 14 E.U. countries are setting their own PNR protocols.
America's VWP partners clearly share our interests and will look for ways to enhance their own security at the same time. In the wake of recent terrorist attacks, European countries have taken steps to reduce radicalization, improve intelligence, increase criminal penalties, impose administrative measures to prevent travel, and enhance information collection and sharing.

5. The Electronic System for Travel Authorization (ESTA) is now in place and has recently been enhanced. It offers the rough equivalent of a visa application, and information obtained through ESTA is checked against the terrorism databases, which are managed by the National Counterterrorism Center (NCTC). Matches have been found, preventing potential terrorists from entering the United States. How could ESTA be further enhanced?

6. Pre-boarding passenger screening offers a number of possibilities. Computer-Assisted Passenger Pre-Screening (CAPPS) was a program implemented on the recommendation of the White House Commission on Aviation Safety and Security in 1997. Using PNR information, CAPPS reportedly identified 9 of the 19 hijackers on 9/11, although by that time the system had been effectively disconnected from the security checkpoint. CAPPS II, an improved version, was abandoned as unworkable. It was replaced by Secure Flight, which relies primarily on matching names with current watch lists.
Israel has historically relied heavily on pre-boarding interviews to screen passengers. The approach, however, is labor-intensive and is more difficult to apply to passenger loads more diverse than those flying on El Al, although in 2001, ICTS, a private security company contracted to interview passengers on U.S.-bound flights using the Israeli approach, correctly identified Richard Reid, the Shoe Bomber, as a person warranting further questioning.
The Transportation Security Administration (TSA) has spent nearly a billion dollars to train and deploy behavioral-detection officers in an effort to identify

high-risk passengers, but the approach remains controversial. Many regard behavioral detection as bogus science, although it may have value as a deterrent. The criticism that behavioral techniques have not led to the apprehension of any terrorists is misleading. In fact, none of the security measures in effect at U.S. airports have led to the apprehension of any terrorists here, and insofar as I can recall, only one terrorist was actually intercepted at a checkpoint abroad. A number of new technologies based on detecting subtle physiological responses to questions or images are in development. We still have no "X-ray" for a person's soul.

Screening programs like TSA's Automated Targeting System (ATS) aim at flagging those who may pose a higher risk. An alternate strategy is to identify populations of passengers unlikely to pose any risk, thereby allowing security officials to more efficiently focus their efforts. An example is TSA's Pre-Check program for trusted frequent fliers. It may be possible for U.S. officials to develop algorithms aimed at identifying travelers entering the United States under the VWP who similarly are likely to pose little risk. The NCTC now works with the State Department and Customs and Border Protection (CBP) to establish screening rules that narrow the screeners' field of view so that they can concentrate on those they should be most worried about.

7. Pre-clearance procedures are being extended to a number of foreign airports. These allow passengers to complete immigration and customs formalities before boarding, but they also provide opportunities for interviews and behavioral observation.

8. Arrival screening and secondary interviews by U.S. Immigration and Customs Enforcement (ICE) and CBP offer the final line of defense before entry into the United States. It has already been recommended by a number of intelligence practitioners and experts that both agencies expand and enhance their intelligence capabilities.[8]

If all else fails, domestic intelligence efforts, which have already detected terrorist plots by foreigners coming here intending to carry out attacks, may thwart future terrorist plots. Arriving terrorists would still have to acquire weapons or explosives, which would increase their risks of exposure.

I, personally, have not done any research to determine precisely how each of these lines of defense might be improved. No doubt, some of the elements mentioned are already being examined by those in Government, but from the perspective of Congressional oversight, it is worth asking whether such examinations are in fact occurring. The challenge will be to integrate them into a National and international strategy aimed at intercepting foreign fighters before they enter the United States and before they return to VWP as well as non-VWP countries

The VWP offers considerable commercial, diplomatic, and cultural benefits. Abandoning the program could overstretch consular office resources and would not necessarily offer improved security. In fiscal year 2012, nearly 19 million people entered the United States under the VWP; in fiscal year 2013, approximately 11 million residents of non-VWP countries applied to enter the United States on non-immigrant visas, of which 9 million were approved and 2 million were refused entry.[9] The application and review process requires extensive documentation by the applicant and extensive investigation by U.S. authorities, including an in-person interview with a consular official. Abandoning the VWP would more than double the current workload. The VWP is not perfect, but neither are non-VWP procedures. The objective should be a level of security higher than the level we had before the VWP was initiated.

The conflicts in Syria and Iraq will continue for the foreseeable future. We will be dealing with their effluent for many years. It is therefore incumbent upon us to develop effective means for preventing the spillover of terrorist violence.

Mrs. MILLER. Thank you very much. I certainly would agree that Visa Waiver is a component and as we look at the thing in the overall. However, I think because of the evolving threat, the chang-

---

[8] Jenkins, Liepman, and Willis, *Identifying the Enemies Among Us*; and Business Executives for National Security, *Domestic Security: Confronting a Changing Threat to Ensure Public Safety and Civil Liberties.*

[9] U.S. State Department, "Worldwide NIV [Non-Immigrant Visa] Workload by Visa Category FY 2013," 2013 *(http://travel.state.gov/content/dam/visas/Statistics/Non-ImmigrantStatistics/NIVWorkload/FY2013NIVWorkloadbyVisaCategory.pdf)*. See also Alison Siskin, *Visa Waiver Program,* Washington, DC: Congressional Research Service, February 12, 2014.

ing circumstances, that really, as I say, has necessitated this hearing today and has certainly been the impetus for many Members of Congress speaking out about this particular program if we try to examine where we have vulnerabilities.

Some—you know, and I appreciate their concern—have actually suggested eliminating this program. I am not in that posture. Although we are trying to understand how necessary the program is for us economically and what we need to do to make sure that we don't have vulnerabilities that we are not really looking at.

I just was trying to take some notes during your testimony. Mr. Dow, you were suggesting in the case of South Korea, for instance, some of the numbers that you were citing were remarkable in the increase of travel that has happened there since they have been a participate in the Visa Waiver. As you mentioned, 23 million travelers last year through the Visa Waiver countries. Those are some really amazing numbers, really.

Also, Dr. Bucci, as you were saying, that we should ask the administration for a list of countries to actually expand the Visa Waiver Program. We may take you up on that. I think that is a very good suggestion. You were talking a bit about Poland, for instance. As I was listening to you, I think you were talking more in bringing them on-board in terms of geopolitical—as a motivator, rather than economic. Although economic certainly, as well.

I guess I would just ask perhaps Mr. Dow or Mr. Bucci, I don't know if you want to suggest any other countries, other than Poland. But what are your thoughts on something like that, of actually using that as a—excuse me—as Dr. Bucci was talking about in regards to Poland. As you were saying, particularly because of what is happening in Russia. To me, I think that is an extremely powerful motivator. More than the economics, quite frankly. But Mr. Dow?

Mr. DOW. I totally agree with Dr. Bucci as far as giving the flexibility to Homeland Security to increase, as they did, to 10 percent. That is how we added 8 Visa Waiver countries that have been very safe. Countries that we would consider important are—in addition to Poland—would be Brazil, Israel, Croatia, Argentina, Bulgaria, Panama, Romana, and Uruguay. There are 9 countries that are very close to those numbers that we are looking at, and a slight change would enable us to look at them.

If you just took Brazil, Poland, and Israel and Croatia and added them, immediately, within 1 year, I guarantee you would have a million new visitors to the United States who would spend $11 billion and 61,000 jobs. So this is a great opportunity. But we have got to have the strict standards you talk about, improve the program as you said, and then look at adding Visa Waiver—to countries the Visa Waiver Program, which would actually increase our security.

Mrs. MILLER. Anybody else want to comment on that?

Mr. BUCCI. Just that any of the countries with which we have treaty alliances, that we are willing to fight together with against a common enemy, should at least be considered for this program. They should meet the standards and preferably have the waiver ability to the higher standard. Because we think that visa refusal rates is not necessarily the best measure of it. We think having a accurate overstay rate metric would be better. Not—and I know the committee really likes the biometric exit thing. We would love to see biometric exit, if we could get the administration to start counting the overstay rate at all, even with the current methodologies, then the expense of a biometric exit would be I think worthwhile.

Right now, until we can get them to do that, adding the biometric requirement, it would be another really expensive program that the administration wasn't using. So I like the idea. But we have got to get the administration to actually do the overstay counting and enforce it. If we could add those things, I think there are several countries that we could get in here that would have great benefit geopolitically in addition to the security.

I love the economic part. But you know what, if it really hurt the security, I would say bag the economics. They agree with me. But it is—right now, it actually helps security. So we should—you know, you don't often get those two coming together. It is nice to utilize it when it does.

Mrs. MILLER. Dr. Frey, it looks like you want to jump in here.

Mr. FREY. I do, yes.

Mrs. MILLER. But I have one other question for you, as well.

Mr. FREY. Okay. Well, let me make a brief point——

Mrs. MILLER. Okay.

Mr. FREY [continuing]. About—just because it is a perfect follow-up from Dr. Bucci's comment.

Security does have to be paramount. In that context, it is worth noting that for potential countries, the Visa Waiver Program has served as a tremendous incentive to raise security standards and begin to cooperate on these issues. To cite just two examples of the countries named, both Poland and Croatia, for example, have already signed and are implementing the information-sharing agreements that we are talking about in anticipation of being qualified for VWP when and if the time comes.

So we are reaping benefits from a security perspective just by holding the carrot out to these countries and saying here are your target, you might as well start meeting it now. These countries have generally done so.

Mrs. MILLER. But what do you make of the fact I mentioned in my opening state that after a recent terrorist attack in Europe, all of a sudden we received quite a bit of information of names that had previously not been on our radar screen here from some of the Visa Waiver countries? You were talking a little bit about these audits that the Department does and that you have been personally involved in. Maybe you can flesh that out a bit. What is your thought on that?

Mr. FREY. Yes, thank you, Chairman Miller.

I think that as you have said and others have said, information sharing and intelligence sharing is the cue to this. To the extent countries are not meeting their obligations or we are finding out after the fact they are not meeting their obligations, there should be measured consequences for doing so. I was not aware of this particular issue. I do know from conversations with former colleagues at DHS and elsewhere that we are getting a number of names.

I heard a—I think a statistic last week during testimony that there were something like 5,500 names provided—known and suspected terrorists provided to DHS via the so-called HSPD6, Known and Suspected Terrorist Information-Sharing Agreement. Of those 2,500 or so were new, folks that were not on our radar. The other 3,000 or so provided additional amplifying data, maybe another name, an alias, a phone number to information we already had.

So I can't speak to this particular example. But as a general matter, yes, countries have signed up to a certain standard of information sharing with respect to both terrorists and criminals, and they ought to be held to that standard. If DHS finds out that they are not or it turns out that there is a gap, then that gap ought to be addressed.

Mrs. MILLER. Really in my last question, a comment really I guess, is that is part of our legislation, of course; is that we do give the Department of—the Secretary of Department of Homeland Security—tools is really what we are looking for. If we find that some of the Visa Waiver countries are not sharing information in the form that we need to be—to have our comfort level where it needs to be, that he has the ability to suspend these countries.

I don't know if any of you have any thought about that portion of our bill. Dr. Bucci.

Mr. BUCCI. Yes, ma'am. I think that is a great idea. They should have that tool. Countries measure their interests in different ways at different times, and they sometimes shift. We saw an explosion of information sharing post-9/11. Everybody realized holy smoke, we really need to get on this. It got much better. Didn't get perfect. After the Charlie Hebdo attacks in France, several of our allies, maybe we should be sharing a little more than we were. They are. That will continue.

But I think having the Secretary of DHS, having that ability to have a stick in addition to a carrot is useful. Used wisely, should keep that level of information sharing high.

Mrs. MILLER. Thank you.

Chairman recognizes my Ranking Member.

Mr. VELA. Thank you, Chairman Miller.

Dr. Frey, I suppose that the reason the travel industry likes the Visa Waiver Program is because it just makes it more efficient for travelers coming over. Can you explain to me exactly what is it that a person traveling from a non-Visa Waiver Program has to go through that makes it more difficult?

Mr. FREY. Thank you. I think—well, my colleague, Dr. Bucci, has already addressed part of that question. But the main inconvenience factor, if that is what you mean by makes it more difficult, is that if you don't have Visa Waiver status—or, frankly, and it is important to clarify that even under Visa Waiver Program status, we are talking about travel to United States under one particular category of visa, the so-called B visa for short-term stays up of to 90 days for tourism or business travel purposes.

So even if you are a Visa Waiver country, citizens from that country who are coming over here to work, to study, or for any purpose longer than 90 days still has to go through the visa process. So we are talking about a subset of travel, not the entire visa system. But certainly for a non-Visa Waiver country, a citizen would have to go make an appointment at the embassy or consolate, fill out the visa application form, submit to an interview, present biometrics, a digital photograph, and fingerprints. Then there is vetting done. That person is ultimately issued a visa.

I think it is worth making a couple of points in that respect, as well. The vetting done under the Visa Waiver Program is precisely the same as the vetting done under the visa program. The additional questions on the visa application relate much more to economic status and whether you have a job to come home to or property that you own rather than are you a security threat. So we can do sufficient vetting based on the information provided by ESTA. So the databases that the—either the State Department or CBP runs the information against are the same and return the same results.

It is also worth pointing out, of course, that for a number of these countries, the United States issues 10-year, multiple-entry visas. So even if you have an interview the first time, you have a 10-year period under which that interview is increasingly out-of-date. Now, the State Department does vetting, recurrent vetting on visa applicants, just as DHS does recurrent vetting on ESTA approvals. So you do have that backstop.

But if someone is putting quite a lot of weight on the interview, even if you accept that it adds security value—and I would agree with my colleagues that compared to all the other benefits of the Visa Waiver Program, it more than makes up for what is in the interview. But even that interview has a fleeting value. Because it is once, the first time, and then you have potentially a 10-year, multi-entry visa.

But just going to make an interview appointment, waiting in potential line at the consulate, et cetera, is what is the inconvenience factor associated with the visa travel for not much more, if any, security benefit. As a matter of fact, I would say not additional security benefit at all.

Mr. VELA. Mr. Dow, I looked at the list of participating countries, and I didn't see Mexico on it. Is Mexico a participating country or not?

Mr. DOW. We work with Mexico already and have the visa situation—visa—they have to have visas in Mexico.

Mr. VELA. Okay. So they don't participate in the program?

Mr. DOW. Right.

Mr. VELA. Okay. Mr. Jenkins, you mentioned that in the future what we are expecting is about 10,000 European fighters going into the Middle East. What is your best estimate as to what we should do to—how do we track them, how do we make sure that when they leave the Middle East and go back to Europe that they are monitored and that for sure we do everything we can to prevent them from coming here?

Mr. JENKINS. So this is—this relates to the previous issue, and in terms of intelligence sharing. The problem that the Europeans—not that I am here to defend Europeans. I mean, intelligence exchange arrangements are very, very complicated. Over a period of time, they also tend to become a bit routine. If it is not a front-burner issue, it takes a while to get lists updated.

I think the avalanche of names seen after the Charlie Hebdo attacks in Paris reflects not simply their increased willingness to share with us, but also their realization that their compilation of those lists and sharing with one another was not at a level where it should be. We are going to depend primarily on them to help us keep track of those names. That is, those are their nationals. We can assist them in this. But we ultimately depend on their ability to do that. So we want to make sure that they have the very best list.

The other areas where we can provide some assistance is on ground borders. Right now, everyone thinks that these people will return via airliners, which is—which has been true thus far. But right now, Turkey is a key to this thing. Because people are coming back from the Middle East into Turkey, and then crossing land borders into Greece or Bulgaria. These are countries—especially Bulgaria, it is a member of NATO, it needs resources. It can use some help in strengthening that land border. So we can help reinforce some of the priorities that the Europeans have already addressed.

Mr. VELA. One last quick question. Of the current 3,000 or the expected 10,000 European fighters, can we tell what percentage of those are from Visa Waiver Program participating countries and which are not?

Mr. JENKINS. By the way, let me clarify here that the 10,000 is not my guess. The 10,000 is a guess by French officials as to what may happen. The number could be less, it could be greater than that. I expect to see these numbers will be on the move. Every revision we have seen, there have been dramatic increases every time.

The bulk of those going from Europe are going from France, Belgium, the United Kingdom, Germany. Less—far less—smaller numbers going from Eastern European countries. So the bulk are going from a handful of Western countries. France recently revised its total up to 1,400 now that are believed trying to go or who have already departed for the Middle East. So it is primarily a handful of Western European nations.

Mr. VELA. Thank you.

Mrs. MILLER. Thank you.

The Chairman now recognizes and welcomes to the committee Mr. Hurd, Will Hurd from Texas, who—the gentleman has spent over a decade as a covert officer in the CIA. We certainly with your background welcome you so much as a new freshman to our committee.

Mr. HURD. Madam Chairman, thank you. Ranking Member, it is always a pleasure.

One of my jobs when I was in—as an undercover officer in the CIA was—my cover job was stamping visas. So I am very familiar with this program. I would like to—you know, my denial rate was pretty high. So I was pretty tough.

One of the purposes of this hearing is to examine the programs and mechanisms that are in place of the Visa Waiver Program and which strengthens homeland security and help us us identify foreign fighters. My first question is to you, Mr. Frey. You talked about these DHA audits. What other controls are there to determine that the countries participating in this are following, you know, the rules and regulations of the Electronic System for Travel Authorization?

Mr. FREY. Thank you for that question, Congressman. I think there are two—it is helpful to think about the Visa Waiver Program operating on two levels; the individual level, and the country level.

To talk about the individual level, that is where ESTA, the Electronic System for Travel Authorization, is coming in. An applicant must go on-line to get authorization to travel, puts in biographic data. Just as recently as November, DHS added additional biographic data that they are collecting. They should be encouraged to continue to evaluate ESTA to look for additional information that will be helpful for a vetting process.

Then that—the traveler will get a red light or a green light as to whether or not they have an ESTA approval. If they do not have a green light, the airline will not board them for a flight.

Mr. HURD. So to be clear, you can't just wake up—I am a Frenchman, I wake up one day, I want to go to New York City. I just can't go to the airport and jump on a plane?

Mr. FREY. That is right. That is precisely right. Prior to ESTA, you could do something very similar to that. That was precisely the reason in 2007 that we implemented the Electronic System for Travel Authorization; to give us advance notice, to allow us to do the advance vetting, so that you couldn't do that as a Frenchman.

Airlines are now fully compliant. Again, while I am sure as in everything it is possible for mistakes to happen, airlines are subject to fines and other penalties if they transmit or transport people without proper ESTAs, just as they are if they transmit and transport people without proper visas.

So that is the individual level. At the country level, the DHS team goes in, reviews the security standards, talks to CT and security officials to get a sense of how things are going, looks at how passports are being issued and, in fact, manufactured and what vetting is done on passport holders, for example, to make sure they are meeting the citizenship requirements and have criminal background checks and all the things these countries implement. Go to the land border, go to the airports to review security procedures and vetting capabilities. So it is a fairly intensive review; one where DHS, along with elements of the intelligence community and, of course, the State Department and potentially the FBI go in and ask these questions.

Mr. HURD. That type of audit, how often does it happen?

Mr. FREY. That formerly happens per the statute at least every other year. It is probably a 6- to 9-month process from beginning to end. In between, DHS has set up a sort-of a continuous monitoring process using its assets overseas, whether CBP or ICE or obviously State Department personnel, and gets reporting on that.

Mr. HURD. For France, the United Kingdom, Germany, Belgium, are you aware of whether this review has been done in the last 6 months?

Mr. FREY. I am not aware of the exact cycle and whether they have been done in the last 6 months.

Mr. HURD. Okay. All right. Thank you.

Dr. Bucci, this question is for you. I guess compare and contrast the information sharing that happens between countries that are part of the Visa Waiver Program and not part of that.

I would welcome, Dr. Frey, your insight and the other gentleman on the panel's insight on this question too.

Mr. BUCCI. Well, it kind of depends on the bilateral agreements. Info-sharing traditionally is done bilaterally. When I was the attaché in Albania, we established an info-sharing regime with them. It was not as intense as this. It was not as routinized as this. So you would have to go across the whole country, Congressman, our whole world, looking at each individual bilateral agreement.

Friendly countries, we usually have some sort of info-sharing or intelligence-sharing arrangement with them. Some it is very little. Some it is pretty extensive. This is probably one of the broadest compilations of information sharing that you will find, other than the very specific, like the Five Eyes is kind of relationships that we have with those very specific countries.

But this is tailored to take care of the traveler, the information that DHS needs to find someone who is traveling with mal-intent. I think that the various programs that are illustrated on that graphic I referred to are pretty extensive, are pretty well-selected to give DHS the information it needs. If it needs to call on other parts of the U.S. Federal Government, fine. But this is a—the Visa Waiver Program gives them a pretty enormous set of tools to find the bad guys if they are coming in this way.

Mr. FREY. Thank you. I would agree with all of that and add a couple points. Just one, in many cases, the Visa Waiver Program builds on already very strong information sharing. You mentioned the Five Eyes. Of course, with the exception of Canada, those countries are all under the Visa Waiver Program. So there are relationships there.

What the VWP does in those cases which is very important, as you said, it institutionalizes those relationships, some of which may be based on personal relationships or—you know, and people obviously rotate to other jobs. This makes it automated, and it makes it institutionalized.

With newer countries—newer members of the program or countries with which the United States has had a shorter relationship, it really is what kick-started the information sharing. So that is what produces, when put together, the real value of the information sharing under the program. Because it is calibrated towards each of these countries and what information they have.

Mr. HURD. Thank you. Thank you.

Mrs. MILLER. Thank you.

The Chairman now recognizes the young lady from Texas, Ms. Jackson Lee.

Ms. JACKSON LEE. Thank you. Good morning. I thank the Chairman very much. I thank the Ranking Member for this very valuable hearing. I recall that this subcommittee, Madame Chairman, and Ranking Member have really been on point on the Visa Waiver issue.

As you may recall, we did a hearing in September 2014. Really, seems as if we have been doing a number of things, and even passed a bill if I recall when we did the border security bill that we were very concerned about the issue of Visa Waiver.

To the witnesses, let me thank you for your testimony and mention that this hearing is more potent probably in this time and era than ever—that we have ever had questions of Visa Waiver Programs. I have seen this over my years of service in the United States Congress. As we note, our friend and ally Turkey, continually in the spotlight because of its border and relationship—or its relationship to Syria. Whether or not it is Denver teenagers leaving and going through Turkey or London teenagers going through Turkey, then we know for sure that foreign fighters can travel, and particularly those who have Visa Waiver structures in their own countries.

I would like to ask unanimous consent to put into the record H.R. 48, Madame Chairman. It is a bill that I hope that we can work on together in the Homeland Security Committee, both this committee, it is to review a—to require a review of the completeness of the Terrorist Screening Database maintained by the Federal Bureau of Investigation and the derivatives terrorist watch list utilized by the Transportation Security Administration and for other purposes.

Mrs. MILLER. Without objection.

[The information follows:]

114TH CONGRESS

1ST SESSION

H.R. 48

To require a review of the completeness of the Terrorist Screening Database (TSDB) maintained by the Federal Bureau of Investigation and the derivative terrorist watchlist utilized by the Transportation Security Administration, and for other purposes.

IN THE HOUSE OF REPRESENTATIVES

January 6, 2015

Ms. JACKSON LEE introduced the following bill; which was referred to the Committee on the Judiciary

A BILL

To require a review of the completeness of the Terrorist Screening Database (TSDB) maintained by the Federal Bureau of Investigation and the derivative terrorist watchlist utilized by the Transportation Security Administration, and for other purposes.

Be it enacted by the Senate and House of Representatives of the United States of America in Congress assembled,

SECTION 1. SHORT TITLE.

This Act may be cited as the "No Fly for Foreign Fighters Act".

SEC. 2. REVIEW OF THE COMPLETENESS OF THE TERRORIST SCREENING DATABASE (TSDB) MAINTAINED BY THE FEDERAL BUREAU OF INVESTIGATION AND THE DERIVATIVE TERRORIST WATCHLIST UTILIZED BY THE TRANSPORTATION SECURITY ADMINISTRATION.

(a) IN GENERAL.—Not later than 90 days after the date of the enactment of this Act, the Attorney General, acting through the Director of the Terrorist Screening Center, shall complete a review, in coordination with appropriate representatives from the Department of Homeland Security and all other relevant Federal agencies, of the completeness of the Terrorist Screening Database (TSDB) and the terrorist watchlist utilized by the Administrator of the Transportation Security Administration to determine if an individual who may seek to board a United States-bound flight or a domestic flight and who poses a threat to aviation or national security or a threat of terrorism and who is known or suspected of being a member of a foreign terrorist organization is included in such Database and on such watchlist.

(b) REPORT.—Not later than ten days after the completion of the review under subsection (a), the Director of the Terrorist Screening Center shall submit to the Committee on Homeland Security of the House of Representatives and the Committee on Homeland Security and Governmental Affairs of the Senate a report on the findings of such review.

Ms. JACKSON LEE. The other purposes includes this question of Visa Waiver. I think that we would be in a strong position to move forward on legislation like that.

Let me focus my questioning, Mr. Jenkins and others who may wish to answer. Please, steer me if I am making a misstatement. But I believe the Terrorist Center Database and the watch list is not created or maintained by DHS. This is done by intelligence agencies; is that correct? So I have a concern that the data sharing from the Visa Waiver Program nations has to be shared with the DHS through the terrorist screening database and watch list.

The premise of my statement is that you are all four here raising important concerns. I know there is a value to the Visa Waiver Program, because I know that Poland for decades has been asking to participate, and others in this program. The long list continues to have countries that wish to be part of it.

So my question is—let me start with Mr. Jenkins. I heard a comment being made at the table that this administration doesn't keep a list. Having served just a few years in the Congress, I can say administrations don't really keep after visa waivers. That is why the United States Congress continues to have these hearings.

So Mr. Jenkins, since we are problem solvers, I would ask—you just heard the premise of my legislation—a greater sharing of the database with the Department of Homeland Security and some infrastructure dealing with Visa Waiver lists, overstays, to really get us in the business of Visa Waiver, making it work, but also protecting the Nation.

Mr. JENKINS. In terms of the management of—the fact that one agency may manage the list, put together, assemble these lists and manage it, should not interfere with other agencies having access. So an ESTA application, however it comes in and is processed, it is checked against the tide and the other lists that reside in other parts of the U.S. Government.

So the fact that DHS is not the manager of this database is not an impediment to checking of names. In fact, names—matches have been found on ESTA applications, and potential terrorists denied entry as a consequence.

Ms. JACKSON LEE. Well, I will follow up with that. It should not be an impediment. But I think there is no intent in my question to suggest that the management be switched. The intent of my question is to indicate that DHS does not manage it. So it is an agency that has responsibility for domestic security. I believe there should be a more structured role for DHS in the sharing—or in the handling of the list. So I always think that we can improve the quickness, the accuracy of the list. I think the Department of Homeland Security should be engaged in that.

Mr. JENKINS. I would certainly agree with that. Here is an area where as I say, Visa Waiver Program is one component. In increasing the intelligence role, the capabilities and intelligence role of both immigration as well as Customs and Border Patrol——

Ms. JACKSON LEE. Yes.

Mr. JENKINS [continuing]. Which are DHS agencies, that is something that has been recommended by other groups already; that these are a line of defense and we can do more of that in that area.

The other thing is in terms of building a National strategy that will bring all of these key players together, agencies within DHS, those within the intelligence community, State Department, and so on, to ensure that these are not isolated separate lines of defense but, in fact, part of a multi-layered system of defense. That, I think, has to be our goal. That is going to take some—this is a big, complicated Government. That takes—that is an issue—to ensure that that is being done is an appropriate role for Congressional oversight.

Ms. JACKSON LEE. If I just may conclude, I will just end on this note. I see my time is over. I thank the Chairman and the Ranking Member for their indulgence.

As we train Customs and Border Protection and Border Patrol Agents always put it in the context of the Constitutional protections that we have, citizens may be caught up in the movement in and out of the country.

But the other point is that I think the premise of the Visa Waiver Program is good, but we live in a different world. The very point that you made I think is an important instruction and one that I think can be modeled in this committee and used with H.R. 48 as a framework to have that gathering of layered coming together of the agencies to make a surefooted way of addressing the Visa Waiver Program, of keeping it, but as well ensuring that it is a program that does not have the loopholes that many of us see.

I thank you for your testimony. I hope, Madam Chairman, that our friend Turkey, our ally, that we can begin to work with them as other countries on some of the challenges that they are facing and some of the challenges that are posed because of their geographic location. I yield back.

Mrs. MILLER. Chairman now recognizes the gentleman from Pennsylvania, Mr. Barletta.

Mr. BARLETTA. Thank you, Madam Chairman.

Dr. Bucci, in your testimony you cite to 2012 GAO testimony and a 2011 GAO testimony report that found that only roughly half of the 36 countries in the Visa Waiver Program at that time were participating in the information-sharing agreements as they pertain to terrorist watch lists or crime. Now, I know these figures have reportedly improved. Do you know how many there are now?

Mr. BUCCI. The last report, Congressman, said that pretty much all of the participating members in the program had now vastly improved in their information sharing and were trending to reaching a level where they needed to be. That is because not everyone is there yet. That is one of the reasons why we support the giving the

Secretary that ability if somebody backs off on that, that he has that stick.

So they are moving in the right direction. I think we can comfortably say now that all 38 members are sharing information. Some are sharing a little more than others. But they are all moving in the positive direction.

Mr. BARLETTA. But not all to the level where we are satisfied that they are sharing all of the information?

Mr. BUCCI. No. It is not 100 percent equal across the board.

Mr. BARLETTA. So I guess Mr. Jenkins talked about the number of European fighters; that they are increasing as we speak. So why would we, or should we—why would we or should we allow any country to participate or not remove a country from the list who are not sharing the information to the level that we are satisfied with the threat to the United States? As we talk with so many European foreign fighters now being—joining ISIS, why would we not remove them or allow them to continue to participate until they do what we need?

Mr. BUCCI. I think we should remove them if they are not meeting that. But I think at that point today that DHS would tell you, and the GAO most recent reports would say, that everyone is reaching that standard. Now, as I say, some are sharing even more. But some of those are countries like the United Kingdom that we have had long-standing intel-sharing agreements that go way beyond anything that is in this program.

So the ones that are exceeding those things—the others are not gonna reach the standard that the United Kingdom has. We don't share that kind of information with them. So at this point, I would agree if there were someone who was being very recalcitrant, not sharing the information—and then the last part, Congressman, I will throw out. In some cases we don't know what they are not sharing. We found out with France all of the sudden hey, they had a whole bunch of people that they were watching that they hadn't told us about. I don't think it was any mal-intent there. They felt that those people didn't rise to the level that they needed to share it. After Charlie Hebdo they realized yes, that was a bad call, they needed to be sharing that. Now they are.

So this kind of thing—and I will be honest with you, the other aspect is that some of this is the result of Mr. Snowden and the revelations that came out there that kind of put a little frost on info-sharing with some of our friendly countries that Charlie Hebdo I think blew the frost off a lot of them and they decided yes, maybe we didn't like that, but we have got to move forward on this to protect ourselves and for them to protect themselves.

Mr. BARLETTA. A July 2013 GAO report revealed that DHS has lost track of over 1 million foreign visitors to the United States.

Mr. Frey, what mechanisms does the Visa Waiver Program have in place to ensure that individuals who enter the United States under the program leave when they are supposed to?

Mr. FREY. Thank you for that question, Congressman. I don't know if it is the right frame—I think what mechanisms does the Visa Waiver Program have in place. The Visa Waiver Program is part of the larger border security entry/exit program the United States has. As such, the Visa Waiver Program sort-of both benefits and in some cases suffers from some of the flaws or gaps in that program.

I agree that—with some of my colleagues here and some of the statements made that DHS needs to produce these overstay numbers and show us the tracking methodology. They haven't to date for a host of reasons. But I think the data that I have seen, some of it at this point dated. But nevertheless, data that I have seen show that Visa Waiver Program travelers, as you might expect, don't overstay in any significant numbers. They come here for their business trip, they come here for their family vacation, whatever it is, and they go home.

Mr. BARLETTA. How would we know that?

Mr. FREY. Well, we know that because DHS does have a biometric—I am sorry—a biographic exit system based on the passenger manifest being submitted to Customs and Border Protection. Because the 99 percent-plus of Visa Waiver Program travelers travel via air, very few will enter or exit the United States via the land border, the system in that case works. To the extent that DHS can take the manifest from the airline, from British Airways going from J.F.K. to London and say oh look, here are the people who left. We saw when they entered; they entered 3 weeks ago. We check them off as they leave.

Now, the system isn't perfect. Partly because there can be and have been, you know, name mismatches. Partly because some airlines, frankly, do a better job than others in giving a complete manifest. But that system is slowly improving. It does need to get better. I think every day it is getting better. But in the Visa Waiver air environment context, I think DHS has got fairly good visibility into who is coming in and in particular who is leaving.

Mr. BARLETTA. That is great. Okay. Thank you. Thank you, Madam Chairman.

Mrs. MILLER. I thank the gentleman.

The Chairman now recognizes the gentlelady from Arizona, Martha McSally. We also appreciate her joining our committee. She has served in the Air Force for 26 years previous to coming from—coming to Congress. She was the first female pilot, fighter pilot to fly in combat, and the first to command a fighter squadron.

So we appreciate you joining our committee. We are looking forward to working with you.

Ms. MCSALLY. Thank you, Madam Chairman. I appreciate it.

Mrs. MILLER. Chairman recognizes.

Ms. MCSALLY. Dr. Frey, to follow up on the previous question, you mentioned that the administration has not reported the visa overstay numbers for a variety of different reasons. Could you go through some of those reasons?

Mr. FREY. Happy to, Congresswoman. Obviously, happy to do so from my perspective. The administration or the Department may have different views of this.

Ms. MCSALLY. You may be more free to——

Mr. FREY. That is true. I think that some of which—some of them I have already discussed. In the air environment, it is a biometric—I mean a biographic system that relies on the airlines to be able to submit the information. In the past that has been problematic. In part, for example, because there have been various airline mergers over the last several years. As a result of those mergers, they have been forced to integrate old IT systems. You know—and that has proven difficult sometimes in interfacing with CBP and getting the appropriate information. That problem I think has been a bit worsened by some of the lower-cost you know, budget carriers that have now been in the market that, again, they are not spending all that much time on these issues, or perhaps as much time as they should.

I think though that the bigger problem, of course, is that the air environment is only part of this. It is a big part for the Visa Waiver Program. But it doesn't address the land border issue. If you really want to have an accurate overstay count, you are going to have to be able to address the land border problem. That from both an infrastructure and a resource perspective has proven to be a very difficult challenge as to how you ensure that folks are being identified and checked off, so to speak, when they depart via land. That has been a problem that DHS has really struggled with.

So my view has always been that even if you move to 100 percent foolproof air exit system—and I think DHS is very close, in the high 90s in terms of its ability to match by air, you are still leaving a fairly large gap in the land border. Until you close that, you are never going to have a true picture of the overstays.

Of course, the final element here is this is all assuming a conversation about people who entered legally. Also I don't want to get—I don't want to—that is a different set of questions and a different set of challenges. But people who came in illegally aren't likely to check out legally in any event, which adds to the overall uncertainty.

Ms. McSALLY. Other perspectives? Any other——

Mr. DOW. I would just like the say that we—DHS has said to us that overwhelmingly the number of people leave. It is less than 1 percent overstay. Even if someone stays 92 days, then they get reported as an overstay. So those numbers.

But we would like to see DHS release these numbers. We think it is very important for Congress to know, and we think that Congress should demand that they get these numbers so we can take a hard look and really understand that is going on.

Ms. McSALLY. Great. Thank you.

Mr. BUCCI. Just real quickly, a lot of the overstays, Congressman, are, you know, students and people here on work visas. Not the VWP kind of travelers who are here for short-term business meetings or vacation. The problem there is you have got to get those institutions who have sponsored those people, either the companies that have hired them or the universities that have accepted them to let you know when they disappear.

Until we get that system going—and I know it has been years and years, and they don't seem to want to get them to do that. That is what really drives your overstay rates for the overall system up tremendously. It is really not the VWP folks.

Ms. McSALLY. Great. Thanks. Turning to another question on—I know there has been expanded data collected from those that are applying. Do you think that is enough? I mean, it is still less than 20 questions versus somebody who has an in-person interview is about 100 questions. Do we need to expand? What sort of additional data would be required if we wanted to do that?

Mr. FREY. Sure, I am happy to take that first. I think that what DHS did in November was good. I think they evaluated what additional data they needed to do appropriate vetting, and that was the answer they came to. I don't think it should stop there. I think they should continue to evaluate, and I think they will continue to evaluate.

But I think that the biographic information provided on the ESTA form, certainly now that it has been expanded, gives you all you need to do the appropriate security vetting. Most of the other—the vast majority of the additional questions on the visa form are not for security vetting purposes. They are for economic immigration purposes; do you have a house, do you have a job, what are your family ties back in the country? So that information is sort-of, kept off from the application when it goes in for security vetting in any event.

So I think the short answer is yes, DHS probably has what it needs now, but that shouldn't stop it from looking for more as the situation evolves.

Ms. MCSALLY. Okay. Great. My time is expired. So if you just have a brief comment.

Mr. BUCCI. Just that this kind of thing never stops. This is gonna be a process we are gonna have to continue to improve as we get better computer analysis capability tying in these other databases. This stuff is gonna go on. This is not something that you pass the law today and we are done. As much as Americans like those kind of solutions, in this case that is not one of those situations.

Ms. MCSALLY. Great. Thank you.

Thank you, Madam Chairman. I yield back.

Mrs. MILLER. Thank you very much.

Just following up on that for my closing comment here, I just wonder if there is any question that we have not asked the four of you, as you have all had a opportunity to review our bill. I am on a mission with this bill. We hope to mark it up and bring it to the full House, full floor at some point here shortly. So if there is something else that we should be doing in there, we would appreciate you telling us at this time, understanding that it is always going to evolve.

Mr. BUCCI. Madam Chairman, I would just say that, you know, what you are doing is right. This is something that vitally affects our security and our economy and our relations with other countries. It warrants the Congressional oversight you are giving it. It is gonna be something that is gonna continually evolve, and should. So the positive way that your committee is looking at this and trying to approach the situation I think is the right answer. We need to keep at this. Because the bad guys are continuing to work at it. We need to, as well.

Mrs. MILLER. Yes. Mr. Dow.

Mr. DOW. We also support strongly any improvements to this system and your bill; we are totally behind it, any way we can help.

One thing that wasn't asked is, what would happen if the Visa Waiver Program was suspended. I will give you an example. In

2002, Argentina was put out of the program, and visitation to the United States dropped 60 percent. So let's take that number and apply it to all Visa Waiver countries. That is $114 billion U.S., 600,000 jobs. Just a view—of almost $50 billion to earn 60,000 jobs.

So I think we have to understand there are two types of terrorism. There is economic terrorism, and there is physical terrorism. I think we have to guard against both. So in closing, we support what you are doing. We think it is absolutely important to continue to strengthen and improve this program.

Mrs. MILLER. Thank you. Anybody else?

Mr. FREY. Sure. I would reiterate that and say that of course any measures—and I understand that that is not the intent here, and I agree with that. It should not be to suspend or terminate the program. Because we would also lose very important security benefits and we would—it had have a significant effect on our close allies in the face of a whole host of threats, including ISIS and foreign fighters, but also including Russia and other things. So I am glad to hear that that is not where we are going.

Because there are sensible reforms. I think the bill in question makes those sensible reforms and does so not losing sight of what has been working in the Visa Waiver Program. So building on what is a very strong foundation. But I guess if you just asked me what was one more thing that needed to change—and I have been saying this for a number of years. In the beginning, I said it somewhat facetiously, but I am increasingly convinced. The name has to change.

Mr. BUCCI. So true.

Mr. FREY. The Visa Waiver Program gives people the wrong impression. It makes it seem like you can—people are waived into the country——

Mrs. MILLER. That is true.

Mr. FREY [continuing]. Without security checks. It is very hard to combat that. Because it takes quite a while to explain here are all the security checks DHS and other do when it is—when it doesn't seem that way because of the name, so——

Mrs. MILLER. Do you have any suggestions on what we should call it?

Mr. FREY. Sure. The one I have always liked is the secure travel partnership program. In part because the section of the 9/11 Commission and Limitation Act that made ESTA and the information-sharing agreements is called the Counterterrorism and Secure Partnership Act of 2007. So I always thought that that was a nice way to phrase it. Because it is, it is about working with secure partners.

Mrs. MILLER. All right.

Mr. Jenkins, do you have any final comment?

Mr. JENKINS. No. I like the title too. But I would extend our—again, the scope. I know the focus here is the Visa Waiver component. But again, to push and make this part of a National strategy where we really emphasize both internally among the agencies in the United States Government, but also externally with our partners on this; that we can utilize all aspects, everything from improving land border security in particularly exposed countries to shaping the expansion of PNR data that is going on right now in

Europe, to Visa Waiver, to expanding the role of CBP and ICE, that should be part of a National and international strategy that gets us into really secure travel.

Mrs. MILLER. Okay. Well, thank you all, gentlemen. I certainly appreciate, the committee appreciates all of you being in attendance today and for your excellent testimony. I think we all learned a lot today. I know I have some ideas of what we want to do with this bill. So I want to thank you all.

Pursuant to Committee Rule 7(e), the hearing record will be held open for 10 days. Without objection, the committee stands adjourned.

[Whereupon, at 11:22 a.m., the subcommittee was adjourned.]

○

www.ingramcontent.com/pod-product-compliance
Lightning Source LLC
Chambersburg PA
CBHW080918290526
45795CB00007BA/2573